SALE, CHESHIRE, IN 1841

Its People and Their Lives

By

John Newhill

First published in 1994 by
Ashton and Sale History Society and John Newhill.
Sales enquiries to the Publications Officer, Ashton and Sale History
Society, 77 Marford Crescent, Sale, Cheshire M33 4DN.

© John Newhill 1994
ISBN 0 9523513 0 7

Typeset by Northern Writers Advisory Services, Sale, Cheshire M33
4DN.

Printed by Intype Input Typesetting Ltd, Woodman Works, Durnsford
Road, London SW19 8DR

CONTENTS

ILLUSTRATIONS

Photographs

Maps

All maps are the work of the author.

Introduction

Over the past ten years or so a number of books have appeared which show Altrincham, Sale, Stretford, and Urmston as they were fifty or even ninety years ago. This is usually done by means of photographs, with some explanatory text. The present book is an attempt to create a picture of the twin townships of Sale and Ashton-upon-Mersey as they were a hundred and fifty years ago, before the arrival of the railway changed them from a rural community into a 'dormitory' town. As no photographs are available from that time (photography had only just been invented), the picture will have to be drawn in words. First I propose to draw a general picture of Ashton and Sale in 1841; then I will take the reader down each road, discussing the buildings and their inhabitants as we go.

"Why 1841?" you will probably wonder. "Why not 1840 or 1850?" There are two main reasons. Firstly, the 1841 census was the first census to list by name all the inhabitants of the country, along with certain other information (approximate age, occupation, etc.). So we know exactly who lived in Sale and Ashton at that time. Secondly, the date happens to be very close to the date of the Tithe Apportionment. This was accompanied by a very large-scale map of the each parish (scale usually 26 and two thirds miles to the inch) and a list of owners and occupiers of all houses and land. By combining the information from both it is possible to construct a detailed picture of Ashton and Sale, and their inhabitants. This picture is like a snapshot taken through the mists of time and offers a firm basis from which further researches may be undertaken either backwards in time or forwards towards the present day.

There are, however, certain difficulties which make the construction of this picture much more difficult than it appears at first sight. (i) There were no 'official' street names or house numbers in Sale until 1867 at the earliest, and in Ashton it was much later before addresses were rationalised. As a result the 1841 census for both townships contains few addresses, and many of the few road names given have changed beyond recognition. (ii) It is also not easy to ascertain the route taken by the enumerators of the census; this is especially true of Ashton, where the houses appear to be listed almost haphazardly rather than in what would appear to be a rational order. (iii) No addresses are given in the Tithe Apportionment and the names mentioned in it do not always tally with those in the census (because of death and change of occupier). (iv) The number of houses listed in the census is 491; the number of houses listed in the Tithe Apportionment is less than 350. (v) One final difficulty is the fact that intermarriage in a small community meant that many families shared the same Christian names and surnames. For example, there were five 'John Kelsalls' in Ashton and Sale in 1841 and all were farmers or agricultural workers. The relationship between people of the same surname is not easy to ascertain, as many families attended non-conformist chapels which no longer exist and whose registers have disappeared. All these factors mean that a certain amount of judgement has to be exercised when working out who lives where. A number of people have been omitted altogether because of the numbers involved. However, I am confident that I have constructed as far as possible an accurate picture of the twin townships of Ashton and Sale as rural communities just before the advent of the railway changed them for ever.

I would like to record my thanks to various people who have given me information which helped to fit pieces of the 'jig-saw' together, and also to Mrs. Jayne Britton and Miss Laura Thompson of Trafford Local Studies Centre for their patience and help when bombarded with many requests over a period of months.

I would like to thank Peter Hughes for giving me the framework of the analysis of occupations in Ashton and also my wife, Jean, for her patience and support on the countless occasions when I disappeared yet again to unearth more facts.

Lastly, I would like to thank Trafford Local Studies Centre for permission to reproduce the photograph of the cottages at Sale Green, and also Peter Hall for allowing me to copy his old photograph of Buck Lane. All other photographs and maps are by myself.

John Newhill
June 1994

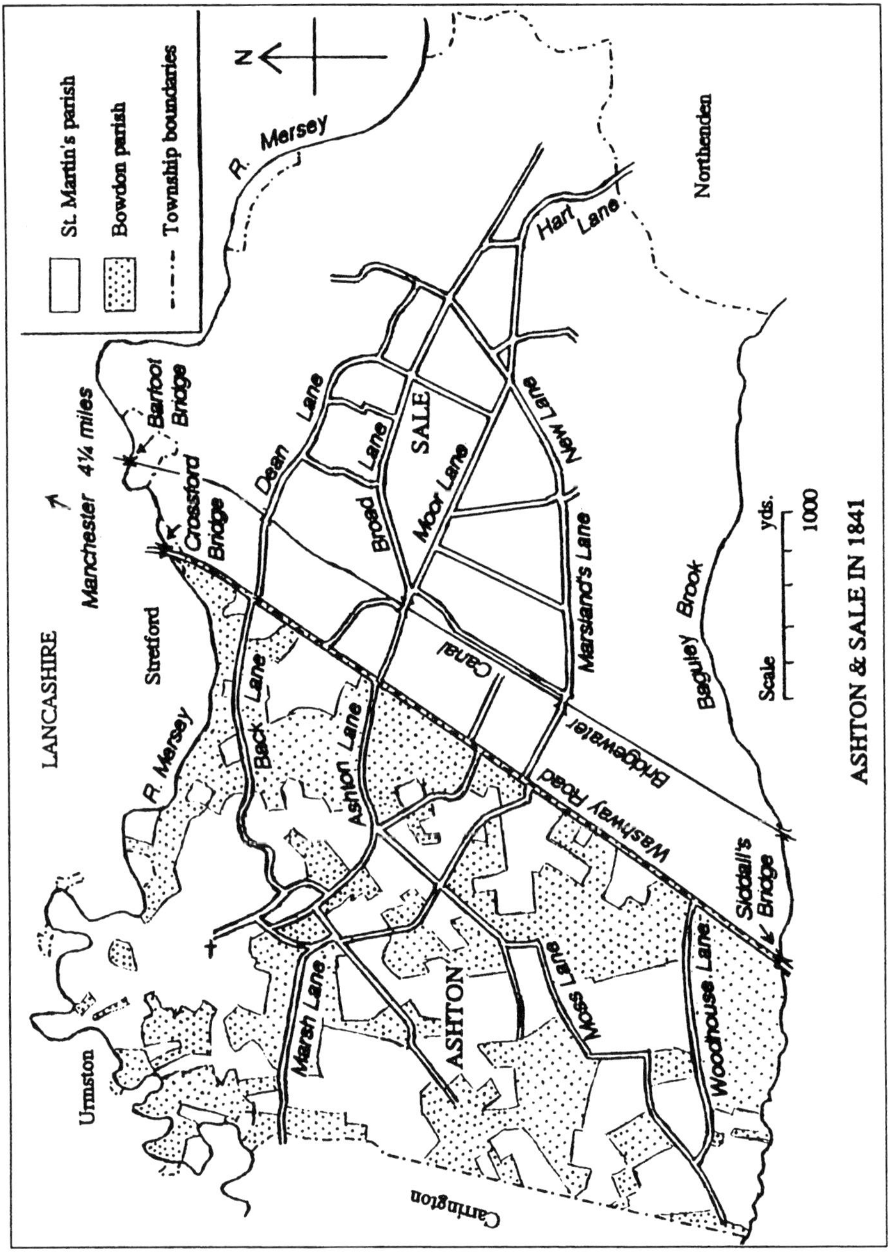
St. Martin's parish
Bowdon parish
Township boundaries
N
R. Mersey
Northenden
Hart Lane
New Lane
SALE
Dean Lane
Broad Lane
Moor Lane
Barfoot Bridge
Crossford Bridge
Manchester 4¼ miles
Marsland's Lane
Canal
Bridgewater
Washway Road
Stretford
LANCASHIRE
R. Mersey
Back Lane
Ashton Lane
Baguley Brook
Scale
yds.
1000
Siddall's Bridge
Woodhouse Lane
Moss Lane
Marsh Lane
ASHTON
Urmston
Carrington

ASHTON & SALE IN 1841

1. Life in Ashton and Sale in 1841

Background

Ashton-on-Mersey and Sale are situated five miles south-west of Manchester, on the northern edge of the Cheshire plain. At street level there are no hills to be seen, but from the tops of several buildings the arc of the Pennines can be seen some 15 miles away to the north and east. In 1841 the atmosphere of Ashton and Sale was far removed from today's urban bustle. Broadly the townships resembled in appearance the rural communities which still remain in the locality, such as Warburton and Dunham – flat fields stretching as far as the eye can see, separated by hedges, and dotted with trees and occasional red-brick or white-washed buildings.

The 1841 census was taken on the night of Sunday, 6th June. At the time Queen Victoria was 22 years of age, having been on the throne for nearly four years.

Township Boundaries

The two townships of Ashton-upon-Mersey and Sale became one urban district in October 1930. Prior to this they had been separated for over a thousand years by the Roman road from Chester to Manchester (now the A56). The Saxons often founded their settlements away from Roman roads, and the two settlements of Ashton (Saxon: "the farm or hamlet of the ash trees") and Sale (Saxon: "by the willows") were each established about a mile from the road, Ashton on the west side and Sale on the east. The fact that the road itself was taken as a boundary points to there being no settlement along the road itself at the time the boundaries were determined, although by the 1800's a number of houses, shops and inns had been built along the road, chiefly on the Ashton side. This was the hamlet of 'Cross Street', which was listed with Ashton in contemporary directories ('Sale' did not merit a mention until Bagshaw's Directory of 1850).

The northern boundary of both townships was the River Mersey (Saxon: "boundary river"), which separated the Saxon kingdoms of Northumbria and Mercia, and later formed the boundary between Lancashire and Cheshire. There were some minor divergences (for example, fields on the 'wrong' side of the river) on the Ashton side; these were probably due to changes in the course of the Mersey over the years. In Sale there were three large 'islands' of Lancashire on the south side of the river at each of the bridges – Crossford Bridge, Barfoot Bridge and Jackson's Bridge. The fact that these 'islands' were at the bridges and also had some right-angled corners may point to this part of the boundary having been man-made, probably dating from the transfer of land from Cheshire to Lancashire which Norman Swain suggested took place in the eighteenth century.

The southern boundary of both townships was a stream which flows westwards into the Mersey. In Sale it is 'Baguley Brook' and it becomes 'Sinderland Brook' when it emerges in Ashton on the west side of Siddall's Bridge (the bridge carrying the A56).

The eastern boundary, between Sale and Northenden, was 'Sale Hedge'. This was originally a stream, a spur of Baguley Brook running northwards into the Mersey. Over the years the stream had dried up and the boundary was marked by a hedge growing in a ditch.

On the western side, between Ashton and the neighbouring parish of Carrington, lay Carrington Moss – a large area of wild, uncultivated land. As there was no natural marker, the boundary here was less easily defined, and seems to have changed over the years. Certainly, Bryant's map of 1831 shows the boundary curving in an 'S', but by the 1840's most of it had become a straight line. The Tithe Map also shows a minor adjustment agreed between Ashton and Carrington in 1845.

Parishes

Although the outer boundaries of the ecclesiastical parishes tallied with those of the civil townships, the position inside these boundaries was rather confusing. Until the formation of St Anne's parish in 1856, the whole of Sale township lay in the parish of St. Martin's, Ashton-upon-Mersey. Yet only half of Ashton-upon-Mersey township was in St. Martin's parish! The other half formed a detached portion of Bowdon parish until 1893. Perhaps it would be more accurate to say 'detached portions', as the distribution of land between Bowdon and St. Martin's resembled a patchwork quilt, with isolated fields sometimes belonging to one parish in the middle of fields belonging to the other parish, and houses next door to each other being in different parishes (see map on p.iv and also section on 'Land Ownership', p.9). The exact boundaries between St. Martin's and Bowdon parish were a source of some dispute, and had to be fixed by the Assistant Tithe Commissioner in 1845.

Roads

The A56 runs between Ashton and Sale in a straight line, roughly from north-east to south-west. This road was originally part of the Roman road from Chester to Manchester and thence to north to Ribchester and east to York; many writers regard it as an extension of 'Watling Street', the Saxon name for the Roman road from Dover to Wales. The road has been extremely busy for over two hundred years. It was turnpiked in 1765, and by 1841 it carried immense quantities of agricultural and gardening produce going to the Manchester markets, much of it from farms round Altrincham and Knutsford. The carts returned with coal and manure (mostly night-soil from the privvies of Manchester). 500 yards to the east of the road and parallel to it is the Bridgewater Canal, which was opened from Stretford through Sale to Altrincham in 1766. Alongside the canal is the railway, which was opened on 20th July, 1849 (N.B. not the 21st, as some writers have quoted).

The other main roads in the area run west-east from Warrington, through Lymm, Carrington, Ashton and Sale to Baguley, Northenden and Stockport. The route via Buck Lane, Glebelands Road and Dane Road must have been important over a thousand years ago, as both the settlements of Ashton and Sale grew up along it. There is a strong local tradition that it was a Roman road, although firm evidence of this has yet to be discovered. One other main road, Brooklands Road, which runs south-east into Timperley, was not built until about 1860.

In 1841 the old traditional road and street names were still in use; most of them were changed and many were lost forever in 1867 when the newly-formed Sale Urban District Council decided to rationalise and up-grade the township's road names. Many 'lanes' such as 'School Lane' and 'Dean Lane' became 'roads' (there were two exceptions), while other 'lanes' such as 'Finch Lane', 'Hart Lane' and 'Northen Lane' disappeared altogether, although several lingered on in colloquial use for a few years. As Ashton was a separate township, the 'lanes' there have remained until today with few changes.

Transport

In 1841 the railway age was just dawning. The first passenger railway in the world had been open for less than eleven years. The main line from Manchester to London had not quite reached Stockport, and the line through Sale to Altrincham was not yet conceived. All land journeys in the two townships therefore had to be made by carriage, on horseback or on foot, depending on one's financial position. The wealthier inhabitants would travel around in their own carriages, although only two people in the 1841 census stated their occupation to be 'coachman'. Farmers and people who owned horses would travel on horseback, while the poorer inhabitants had to walk everywhere. In the nineteenth century a walk of three or four miles to work or to church was quite the normal thing.

A number of stage-coaches provided transport to Manchester, Northwich, Warrington and Chester. The *'Rapid'* and the *'Velocipede'* ran to Chester and back on alternate days. Each day one left Sale not long before twelve and the other arrived from Chester about three in the afternoon. The *'Nettle'* ran to Northwich and the *'John Bull'* to Warrington and back. There were also three 'omnibuses' a day between Altrincham and Manchester. Finally, there were boats on the Bridgewater Canal, two a day to both Manchester and Liverpool.

Sale Moor

What is today the 'centre' of Sale was uncultivated moorland until the enclosures of 1805-7. This was 'Sale Moor', where all the inhabitants had an equal right to graze their pigs or horses. There is a strong tradition that some of Bonnie Prince Charlie's men stole the rector of St. Martin's horse from the Moor in 1745. Later it was used as a training ground for soldiers of the Manchester garrison at the time of the Napoleonic Wars. Roughly triangular in shape, it was almost a sixth of the total area of Sale, covering the land between Washway Road (from School Road to Raglan Road) on the west, Northenden Road on the north, and Marsland Road on the south. The Enclosure Award of 1807 parcelled out the land, giving it to existing land-owners in proportion to their current holdings. Although the poorer people received nothing in return for their lost rights, the newly-enclosed area created work as it was transformed into excellent pasture and highly-productive arable land.

Flooding

The land on both sides of the Mersey was low-lying and very susceptible to flooding. These floods caused many problems until the opening of the Manchester Ship Canal in 1894, when the waters were used as a supply for the canal. Flooding in winter resulted in fields covered in sheets of ice, upon which the inhabitants were able to skate and play games. The floods certainly extended as far as the cellars of the Priory in Sale, and Barracks Farm in Ashton.

Population

Year	Ashton	Sale
1831	974	1104
1841	1105	1309
1851	1174	1720
1931	9704	18367

The above table illustrates how the coming of the railway in 1849 affected the two townships in different ways. Between 1841 and 1851 the population of Ashton increased by 6%; in the same period, the population of Sale, where the railway station was located, increased by 31%. By the time the two townships were joined together, the population of Sale was nearly double that of Ashton.

Lords of the Manor

The title of 'Lord of the Manor' for Ashton was held by George Grey, the 6th Earl of Stamford and Warrington, who lived at Dunham Hall. The title of 'Lord of the Manor' for Sale was purchased by the Worthington family of Altrincham when they bought Sale Old Hall from Captain John Moore around 1840. Although these titles had become virtually prestige titles by the middle of the nineteenth century (Manorial Courts had long ceased to operate), the social hierarchy was strictly maintained. One small example – shopkeepers (in their white aprons) came running out into the street to serve a member of the 'gentry' in his or her carriage.

Local Government

Each township was independent and had to rely on its own resources; there were no funds from central government or the County Council. The functions of the Manorial Court had been taken over by the Township Vestry, a committee made up of rate-payers and land-owners. The leading citizens took turns to occupy the 'chair' and on 3rd March, 1841 we find the Rev. John Hunter chairing the meeting to elect the officers for Sale Township for the following twelve months. The officers were all unpaid, and were elected by a system of voting (the number of votes each individual had depended on the amount he or she paid in rates and therefore depended on the size of the property owned). The various posts tended to be rotated round a fairly small group. Instead of paying one sum of money per year in rates to the town council (as is the modern custom), rate-payers had to pay at least three sums to different people, as we shall see below.

Overseers of the Poor – John Brogden, Joseph Hampson, Richard Howarth, Paul Marple and John Whitehead (John Brogden was a landowner, not a resident at the time). These officers levied the Poor Rate and saw to its distribution. Often two rates were levied in one year and the Township Minutes tell us that in 1848 a rate of 9d. in the £ was raised in May, and 4½d. in November. The total income for the year was £404.11s.6½d. (£404.58p).

Surveyors of the Highways – Samuel Alderley and Thomas Renshaw. It was their duty three times per year to survey all the roads in the township (except for the Turnpike) and organise labour to repair them. We have no figures for 1841, but in 1835 the Highway Rate raised £257.7s.6d. (£257.38p) and the money spent was £224.5s.3d. (£224.26p).

Assessors of Assessed Taxes – John Cordingley and Peter Tyrer. This office is not mentioned in any book on local history. Presumably the assessors helped with the calculation and collection of rates and taxes.

Churchwardens – Robert Marsland and Joseph Nield. It was their duty to maintain the fabric of the parish church and pay for bread, wine, and instruments for the services. This they did by levying a 'church rate', and their rate-books usually served as the basis for raising the other rates (Poor Rate and Highway Rate).

Constables – John Sutherland and William Cookson. They had been elected in October, 1840, as the Constables were elected every October. Theirs was an unpopular job, as they were responsible for keeping order in the township. They were responsible for the maintenance of the town lock-ups and stocks, the apprehension of criminals and miscreants, and the removal of strangers and beggars from the parish.

Sparrows seem to have been a particular nuisance at the time and the constables were empowered to kill sparrows for the sum of 1d. for each hen and ½d. for a cock or young bird. There was also an official mole-catcher – Jonathan Brownhill. Two years previously his salary had been reduced from £6.15s.0d. (£6.75p) per year to £3.0s.0d. and early in 1842 his services were dispensed with altogether.

Churches

In 1841 there were only two churches in Ashton. One was St. Martin's, which was the parish church for half of Ashton and the whole of Sale. The other church was the New Chester Wesleyan Methodist Chapel on Washway Road.

There were four churches in Sale, all non-conformist. These were Cross Street Chapel (the Unitarian Chapel in Chapel Road), the Independent (Congregational) Chapel near Sale Bridge, the Wesleyan Methodist Chapel in Broad Road and the Primitive Methodist Chapel on Northenden Road.

In view of the fact that the one parish church was situated at the extreme north-west of the two townships, it is not surprising that many of the inhabitants were non-conformists.

Tithes

For over a thousand years from the time of King Offa of Mercia, 'Tithes' had been paid at Easter to the local vicar or rector. This 'ancient and laudable custom' (to quote the pre-amble to the Tithe Apportionment) required inhabitants to pay a tenth of their income in kind – hay, lambs, chickens, apples, and even beer. The system was inconvenient for both the payer and the recipient, and in 1836 the Tithe Commission was set up to convert these taxes into money. 11,800 parishes (79% of the total in England and Wales) were surveyed, and every field and house in them listed and mapped. These maps, usually at a scale of 26 and two thirds inches to the mile, are often the first accurate large-scale maps of a parish. The accompanying hand-written 'Tithe Apportionment' listed each house and field, with the owner, occupier, area and usage. Large parishes were often split into their constituent townships, as in the case of Sale and Ashton.

The dates of confirmation and amounts of the Tithe Awards for Ashton and Sale are:

Ashton (Bowdon parish)	21st Nov. 1838	£156	p.a.
Sale	20th Apl. 1844	£489	
Ashton (St. Martin's)	27th Nov. 1847	£210	

To obtain an overall picture for Ashton, therefore, we have to add together the figures for the two portions of the parish (many inhabitants held or rented land in both parts). This is made impracticable by the 9 years separating the two awards, as some owners had died and properties had changed hands in the intervening period. There is, however, a separate list of the properties (with owner, occupier, area) for both Ashton and Bowdon parts prepared for the Tithe Commissioners, and dated 1st September, 1845. This list was made in an effort to settle the boundaries between St. Martin's and Bowdon parishes, and has been taken as the basis for the figures in this book.

The rector of St. Martin's received all the tithes for Sale and half of those for Ashton St. Martin's, the remaining half of the latter going to the Earl of Stamford and Warrington. £5 of the tithes for the Bowdon section went to the rector of Bowdon and the rest to the 'improprietor'.

Land Ownership

The areas of the two townships were:-

Ashton (St. Martin's)	831 acres 1 rood 18 poles
Ashton (Bowdon)	780 acres 0 roods 35 poles
Total	1611 acres 2 roods 13 poles
Sale	1981 acres 1 rood 20 poles

The pattern of land ownership differed in the two townships. The table below lists the ten largest land owners in each.

Ashton

William Wainman	327	acres
Earl of Stamford	251	
Thomas Whitelegg	142	
Rev. John Hunter	115	
John Smith exors.	116	
John Gallemore	72	
William Shawcross exors.	62	
Mary Ashton exors.	41	
Robert Newton	40	
John Newton	38	

Sale

John White	291	acres

George C. Legh	187
Samuel Brooks	166
Lawrence Wright	154
Mary Woodiwiss	100
Joseph Taylor exors.	77
John Baxter exors.	68
Joseph Clarke exors.	61
Barbery Shawcross	46
Edmund Howarth	46

In Ashton virtually all the large properties were occupied by their owners. Although the Earl of Stamford lived four miles away, all his land was on long-term lease to families who lived on the property for generations, and who may therefore be regarded as 'owners'. Two of the properties administered by executors were also occupied by relatives and inheritors of the property. In Sale the position was very different. Not until we reach the tenth in the table (Edmund Howarth) do we find an owner actually living on his property.

An often-repeated statement is that Samuel Brooks, the Manchester banker, purchased 515 acres of Sale (a quarter of the total township) in 1829. This is supported neither by the above figures nor by the Land Tax Assessment for 1830. Further research may reveal whether the '515 acres' included land in neighbouring townships.

The strange division of land between St. Martin's and Bowdon parish in Ashton (see map, p.iv) deserves further comment. It is possible that certain people in Bowdon wished to retain ownership of some of their lands in Ashton when the parish of St. Martin's was created out of Bowdon parish around 1300 A.D.; this, however, does not seem to have been the case because of two reasons. It would be reasonable to expect that by 1844 some person in Bowdon had retained ownership of at least one or two acres in Ashton, or, possibly, that the pattern of land-ownership in Ashton would show some owners having land solely in the Bowdon section as a legacy of Bowdon ownership. Neither of these applied. Without exception all the people who owned land in Ashton had lands in both St. Martin's parish and the Bowdon portion. For example, Major Wainman, the largest land-owner, had 162 acres in St. Martin's and 164 acres in Bowdon parish; the Earl of Stamford had 82 acres in St. Martin's and 169 acres in Bowdon. This pattern was repeated right down to the owners of a few acres and makes the situation seem even more puzzling to us today.

Canal Bridges. Before the building of the railway, the three canal bridges were like this one at Agden, near Lymm. (Photograph by author.)

Occupations

The following table gives a break-down of the occupations listed in the 1841 census. It was originally intended for this book but was first published in the *Surname Index of the 1841 Census for Ashton-on-Mersey & Sale*.

	ASHTON		SALE	
	Total	Born in Cheshire	Total	Born in Cheshire
Agriculture				
Agricultural Labourers	108	98	105	95
Farmers	37	29	49	43
Gardeners	9	9	12	7
Nurserymen	1	1	3	1
Total (*see notes*)	155	137	169	146
Trades				
Blacksmiths (incl. 1 apprentice)	4	4	5	3
Brewers	1	–	1	1
Builder	1	1	–	–
Bricklayers (incl. 1 apprentice)	–	–	5	5
Butchers	1	1	2	–
Cabinet maker	1	1	–	–
Cooper	1	–	–	–
Cordwainers (incl. 1 apprentice)	–	–	2	2
Fustian cutters (incl. 2 apprentices)	8	1	4	4
Grocers/drapers	2	2	2	–
Hot platers	3	3	1	1
Hatters (incl. 1 apprentice)	2	2	3	1

	ASHTON		SALE	
	Total	Born in Cheshire	Total	Born in Cheshire
Joiners	2	2	3	2
Painters/printers	1	1	2	–
Publicans & inn-keepers	4	2	2	2
Ropemaker	–	–	1	–
Saddlers	2	2	–	–
Shoemakers	5	3	10	8
Shopkeepers	1	1	3	3
Silk weavers	2	1	2	2
Slaters	1	1	3	3
Tailors (incl. 3 apprentices)	4	3	2	2
Upholsterer	–	–	1	1
Weavers (see notes)	2	2	17	13
Wheelwrights	3	–	3	3
Total	51	33	74	56
General				
Boatmen	1	1	3	1
Brickmakers	2	2	1	1
Carriers/carters	2	2	1	1
Charwoman	1	1	–	–
Coachmen	1	–	1	1
Coal dealers	–	–	4	3
Dressmakers/ seamstresses	6	4	–	–
Gamekeeper	1	1	–	–
Horsekeeper	1	–	–	–
Labourers	–	–	16	14
Oil merchant	–	–	1	–
Police constable	–	–	1	1
Toll-bar keeper	1	–	–	–
Warehousemen	–	–	2	–
Washerwomen	2	2	–	–

	ASHTON		SALE	
	Total	Born in Cheshire	Total	Born in Cheshire
Total 18	13	30	22	
Professional				
Agents	2	–	–	–
Army (retired)	–	–	1	–
Auctioneer	1	1	–	–
Banker	–	–	1	–
Barrister	–	–	1	1
Civil engineer	–	–	1	–
Clergymen	2	–	–	–
Commission agents	1	1	1	–
Commercial clerk	–	–	1	–
Independent means	31	14	24	12
Merchants	–	–	2	–
School teachers	–	–	6	4
Smallware dealers	1	1	1	–
Solicitors	1	1	1	–
Surgeon	–	–	1	1
Total	39	18	41	18
Servants – male	71	62	53	40
female	77	54	77	48
Total	411	317	443	330
Wives	154	122	187	156
Children (see notes)	488	445	603	550
Others (see notes)	52	35	75	57
TOTAL POPULATION	1105	919	1309	1093

Notes

Agricultural Workers – Many of the farmers had 'servants'; these are included in the total number of servants on this page. However, these servants would certainly have had to help on the farm. The total number of farmers' servants was 140. It is interesting to note that the 43 farmers in Sale had only 39 servants between them whereas the 37 farmers in Ashton had 101!

Weavers and Fustian Cutters – We see the remnants of a cottage-weaving industry. There were four silk weavers and nineteen other weavers. Many of the latter would be garth-weavers, who wove straps and girths for horses. The twelve fustian cutters cut loops in cloth with a knife to make velvet.

Professional – One stipendiary magistrate is not listed. He and his family lived at Sale Priory and were away from home on the night of the Census.

Children – Dividing the number of children by the number of wives gives an average number of children per family (3.6 in Ashton and 3.2 in Sale). This is a very approximate figure, as some of the farmers were widowers, and some of the children had left home and were working in service or as apprentices. The figure for 'children' includes a few grandchildren and a number of children who were grown-up, but had no separate employment listed in the Census.

Others – These are people difficult to include elsewhere, for example, men listed as 'lodgers', women listed as 'widows', 'taking in lodgers', nurse children, elderly relatives not 'of independent means' and also paupers.

Place of Birth – As Ashton and Sale were situated right on the north boundary of Cheshire, it is not surprising that 17% of the population were born outside the county even before the opening of the railway.

Farms
In the 1841 census 37 people claimed to be 'farmers' in Ashton, and 49 in Sale. A number of these may be discounted, as they rented only one or two fields, and were really market gardeners or even agricultural labourers.

The acreages of the farms in Ashton and Sale were as follows:-

	Ashton	Sale
over 60 acres	6	7
50-60	3	2
40-50	4	3
30-40	5	6
20-30	6	6
10-20	6	5
below 10	5	7

6 of the farms in Ashton were owned by the farmer, 5 were part-owned and the rest were rented or leased.

4 of the farms in Sale were owned by the occupier, 3 were part-owned and the rest were rented or leased.

The largest farms in each township were as follows:-

Ashton

Grange Farm (Robt. Newton, jun.)	127	acres
Macum Farm (James Royle)	107	
Smith's Farm (Charles Smith)	102	
Siddall's Farm (Thomas Siddall)	74	
Moss Farm (Thomas Bancroft)	60	

Sale

Bridge Farm (Robert Marsland)	154	acres
New Sale Hall (Sarah Whitelegg)	124	
Wallbank Farm (Samuel Alderley)	116	
Baxter's Farm (Peter Brown)	68	
Woodiwiss's Farm (John Hampson)	67	

The Tithe Apportionment gives the usage of each field, and this enables us to have a clearer idea of the sort of farming carried out at the time.

	Arable Acres	Meadow Acres
Ashton St. Martin's	561	157
Ashton Bowdon parish	509	176
Sale	1300	500

We therefore see that the ratio between growing crops and keeping cattle was approximately three to one. The crops were principally oats,

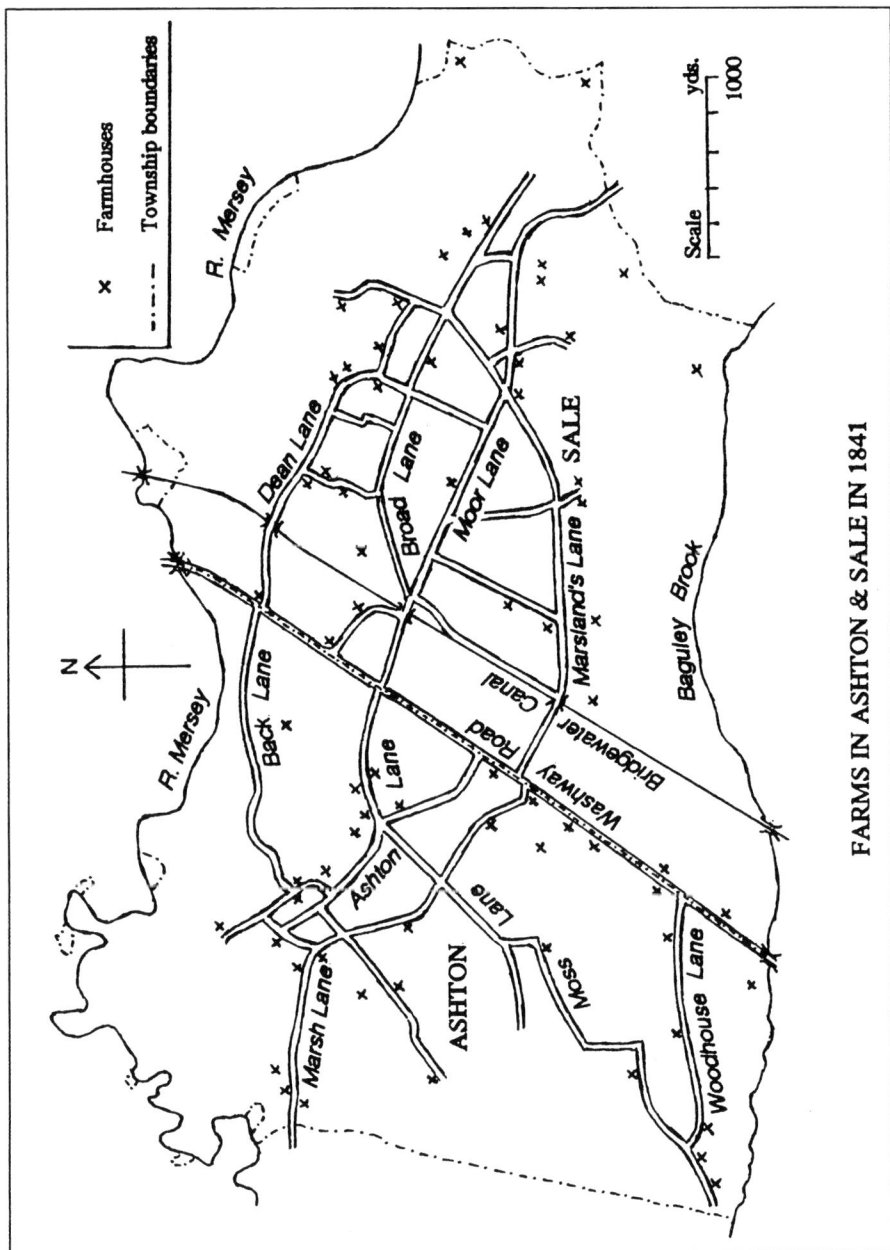

FARMS IN ASHTON & SALE IN 1841

barley, some wheat, and a large amount of vegetables (the latter especially among the occupiers of smaller holdings).

The 1851 census gives us an idea of the number of labourers employed by each farmer to run his farm. The numbers vary and must have depended to a certain extent on the type of farming carried out. Robert Marsland said he had 4 labourers to farm 140 acres; Samuel Alderley had 6 men for 114 acres; Thomas Richardson had 2 men for 54 acres; William Brown on the other hand had 3 labourers for 22 acres.

Schools

There were two township schools, one in Ashton and one in Sale. Both were spartan affairs with stone floors and very little heating. The number of pupils in each was approximately 50. The Ashton school was run by John Fletcher, and the Sale one by James Warren. There was also a school for fee-paying young ladies run by Jane Bellott on Cross Street. The gentry of Ashton and Sale sent their children away to boarding school rather than have them attend the township schools.

Living conditions

Life was hard, especially for the poorer classes. There was no electricity or gas, and many of the things we take for granted today – television, radios, washing machines, fridges – did not exist. Cars, bicycles and cigarettes were also unknown. Beef was 3p/lb, milk ½p a pint, bread 3½p for a 4lb loaf, and beer 5p a gallon. Shoes cost 15p a pair, and a new suit about £1.12½p. It cost ½p to send a letter by the newly-established 'Royal Mail' (prices in decimal money).

Wage rates were equally low. A farm labourer in Cheshire earned about 63p per week. Out of this he had to pay his rent (25-27p per week) and keep his family. There was no unemployment pay, sick pay, or old age pension. Anyone who could not manage on his or her income was a 'pauper' and depended entirely on a few pence per week donated by the Overseers of the Poor. On the other hand, there was no income tax in 1841 – it had been suspended in 1816. It was, however, re-introduced in 1842.

Mortality

An analysis of the burials over ten years at St. Martin's Church shows the high level of infant mortality in 1841. During the ten years 1836-1845 there were 578 burials. Of these 251 (43.4%) were under the age of 5; and 142 (24.6% of the total) were 'infants' (babies up to two or three months old). Death and disease had no respect for position; the same year (1846) saw the death of the rector's infant daughter and also the death of the 15-year old daughter of Major Wainman of Woodheys Hall.

Ashton New Hall (see p.46). (Photograph by the author.)

2. Washway Road

If we stand at the southern edge of Sale (the bridge over Sinderland Brook just north of the 'Pelican' inn) and look towards Manchester, we can see Washway Road (the A56) stretching out almost in a straight line. We cannot quite see the northern boundary, the River Mersey, over two miles away. Nowadays the road is lined by buildings – houses, pubs, shops, office blocks, garages, etc. – for the whole of the distance. In 1841 the traveller would have seen fields on either side containing wheat, oats, vegetables or grazing cattle, with a few buildings dotted here and there. The eye can just about see clearly to Marsland Road, which is exactly one mile from the bridge. In this mile there were only nine buildings on the Ashton side of the road and five houses plus two farms on the Sale side. This part of Washway Road in fact remained undeveloped until the 1930's. The heavy traffic along the road in the nineteenth century consisted mostly of carts and cattle, with the occasional brougham, landau or trap (see p.3). The road was the widest in Sale, about the same overall width as it is today. The actual roadway was, however, narrower than the present road, with wide grassy verges on each side.

Sinderland Brook to Marsland Road

The bridge carrying the A56 over Sinderland Brook is 'Siddall's Bridge'. The Siddall family lived in Woodheys Hall, the large mansion just north of the bridge on the Ashton side of the road. There are records of 'Richard Siddall of Woodheys' in 1671 and 'William Siddall of Washway' in 1742. The hall was set back from the road in its own grounds and a driveway connected it to the main road. It was the largest house in Ashton, and its occupiers were acknowledged as leaders of the community, although the title of 'Lord of the Manor' belonged to George Grey, the sixth Earl of Stamford and Warrington, who lived at Dunham Hall three miles to the south. At some time before 1780 the hall came into the hands of the Wainman family, and in 1841 the hall was the home of Captain (Brevet Major) William Wainman of the Royal East Kent Regiment (the 3rd of Foot, the 'Buffs'), who lived there with his Yorkshire-born wife, Jane, and their four young children. Seven servants looked after the family and the house. Woodheys Hall seems to have been known locally first as 'Siddall's Hall' (it is shown as 'Siddall Hall' on Burdett's 1777 map of Cheshire) and later as 'Wainman's Hall'. The Hall was demolished soon after 1930 to make way for the building of the houses in Clough Avenue and Avonlea Road. In addition to the Hall, William Wainman owned a fifth of the total area of Ashton, including much of the land between Sinderland Brook and Moss Lane.

Walking north from the bridge we would see fields along the left-hand side of the road until we came to the end of Woodhouse Lane. Here was the Old Toll House, built about 1775; on Burdett's map the toll-gate is called 'Washway Gate'. In 1841 it was the home of a gardener, 56-year old Abraham Goodier, and his five children aged seven to twenty. It seems that he also took tolls, as ten years later we find the occupant of the house described as 'toll-bar-keeper' rather than 'gardener'. On the opposite corner of Woodhouse Lane was 'Lane End House', a house and garden rented by 30-year-old Samuel Goodier, possibly a nephew of Abraham. Also living in the house were Samuel's father and mother, three young men called Goodier (presumably brothers and a cousin) and a 10-year-old girl described as 'a servant'. The census describes Samuel's father, James, as a man of 'independent means'; although he lived with his son, he owned a house in Ashton village which was rented out. The Goodier family had lived in Ashton for over 200 years.

250 yards north of Woodhouse Lane was the farm of John Heywood. He lived with his wife, four young children, and two servants. John rented his house and nine fields from three different people, most of it from the Owen family who leased the land between Woodhouse Lane and the modern Fownhope Road from the Earl of Stamford. Ann Owen was the oldest member of the family. Her husband had died in 1834, and she lived with her son James (a farmer) and her daughter in a house built around 1750, which is still lived in today (just south of Selsey Avenue). Ann was 64; she died a few weeks after the census was taken and the house and land were taken over by another of her sons, John. There were four houses between the present-day Fownhope Road and the end of Harboro Road. The first house was the home of one of Ann Owen's other sons, Robert. He was a farmer, born in 1804, and lived with his wife, two very young children and one 10-year-old 'servant'. The second house was occupied by Nancy Hamnett, a widow of independent means. The third group of houses was named 'Woodcourt'. They were in fact the 'poor houses' owned by

Ashton Township, and the 17 inhabitants included John Irlam, an 80-year-old agricultural labourer, with his wife, three children and three grandchildren, plus three agricultural labourers, and two female paupers. John Irlam died 4 weeks after the census was taken. The last house, at the corner of Harboro Road and Washway Road, was 'Brook House', so called because of the stream which flowed under the main road and ran right through the garden. The stream was Button Brook ('The Fleam'), which started in the region of Button Lane (in Northenden) and, after going under the canal and Washway Road, turned northwest and finally joined the River Mersey near the end of the modern 'Carrington Spur'. Brook House was the home of John Bythell, a 68-year-old farmer. He had four servants (aged from 15 to 70) and rented six fields from the Earl of Stamford.

If we return to Siddall's Bridge and look at the Sale side of the road, the first property was Washway Farm; the farmhouse was at right angles to the road, about halfway between the bridge and Woodhouse Lane (it is interesting to note that there was another 'Washway Farm' situated about the same distance south of the bridge in Timperley parish). The tenant of the Sale farm was 34-year old Joseph Hampson, who lived with his wife Deborah, their six children and two servants. His farm land (some 53 acres) occupied most of the area on the east side of the road from Sinderland Brook almost to the next farm, which was situated 500 yards further along the road from Washway Farm. In the 1851 census we find that Joseph Hampson was now a grocer and provision-dealer on Cross Street. The next farm to Washway Farm was New Farm; one source states that it was built when the Bridgewater Canal cut the Vaudrey estates in two. It was rented by Richard Howarth, a man in his fifties, who lived with his wife Martha and a grown-up daughter. In 1841 Richard was one of the Township Overseers of the Poor, as was his neighbour, Joseph Hampson. Two male servants and a labourer also lived at the farm, which covered 59 acres. A stream ran down this part of Washway Road on the east side. Starting near the Bridgewater Canal it ran westwards towards the main road, and then down the side of the road for nearly half a mile, finally emptying into Sinderland Brook. This meant, of course, that the two farms on the east side of the road had to have bridges to give access.

Opposite Ann Owen's house was the cottage of Thomas Aldcroft, a gardener. Between his house and Raglan Road was a very large pond, roughly on the site of the present Baptist Church. It seems that the pond was on the site of an old marl pit, as the area was referred to in the 1851 census as 'Big Pit'. Raglan Road as we know it did not exist, but there was a track which ran along the line of Raglan Road for a short distance and then turned south, skirting the pond, which lay between it and the main road (the track is still there at the side of the church). In a small cottage along this track lived James Howarth, the son of Richard and Martha of New Farm. James lived with his wife Sarah and their three small children. He was an agricultural worker, presumably helping on his father's farm. At the end of the track was a house which was empty in 1841, but which was occupied by a Martin Just in 1844. Nearby were the house and outbuildings of Richard Smalley Yates, nurseryman and fruiterer. Richard was born in Manchester in 1807 and lived with his wife Alice, their two babies, one female servant and a staff of four gardeners. In addition to his nursery (consisting of five rented fields), Richard had a confectionery and fruit business at 3, St. Ann's Square, Manchester. The nursery was later expanded, becoming known as 'Sale Heys Nursery'. Returning to the main road, there was a house a few yards north of the track. This was the home of 48-year old James Hamnett, his wife Anne and their two servants. James was also a nurseryman, renting four fields round the house. From here right up to Marsland Road there were fields and market gardens. Opposite the end of Harboro Road (now blocked off), Button Brook ran under Washway Road as mentioned above.

As described on p.4, the area between Raglan Road and School Road was 'Sale Moor' until the enclosures of 1807. Before this date it had been uncultivated common land, available to everyone for grazing pigs, cattle, or horses.

Marsland Road to School Road

Starting again on the Ashton side of the road we would see two houses just north of the modern Harboro Way. Here 29 people lived, including William Renshaw, a 36-year old farmer. Other inhabitants included his mother, two widows, a seamstress, three agricultural labourers and a carter, with their families. Further up, at the corner of Barkers Lane, was a row of five houses also owned by William. They were leased to James Hamnett, who sub-let them to various people, including a commission agent. Next to the houses was New Chester Wesleyan Methodist chapel, opened in June, 1839 (in 1867 it would be superseded by a new chapel built in Barkers Lane behind the first one). In 1841 from here right up to Ashton Lane, there were fields belonging to Martha Faulkner of Altrincham. The largest field, next to the houses and chapel, was called 'Fighting Cocks' and was possibly the scene of cock fights in the past. By the time of the Tithe Apportionment we find William Renshaw's brother, Jeremiah, had rented a new house built on the roadside.

Returning to the Sale side of the road, we would see a terrace of 8 houses at the corner of Marsland Road and Washway Road. These were known as 'Sale Terrace' and were rented by Sarah Keighley ('Keeling' in the Tithe Apportionment) from a George Robinson, presumably a descendant of the Robinson family who formerly owned the land round Barkers Lane. In addition to Mrs. Keighley the inhabitants included a painter, a solicitor (with their families) and another lady of independent means with her two servants. It is interesting to note that none of the people living in Sale Terrace were born in Cheshire; in fact, in 1841 most of the inhabitants of Sale who were born outside Cheshire lived along Washway Road and Cross Street. Almost next door to Sale Terrace was another row of houses. This was 'New Chester', listed in contemporary directories as a separate hamlet. The houses were leased by 45-year old John Brownhill, who lived in one of the houses with his two teenage children and two servants. He was a provision-dealer and beer-seller – this was later the 'Vine' inn. 56 other people lived in the terrace; they included a number of widows and agricultural workers with their families. One of the widows, Mary Aldred, was a charwoman, but also rented a field in the vicinity, presumably to keep a few pigs and hens.

Roebuck Lane was merely a track leading down to the canal, and nearly halfway along the south side was a large house in its own grounds. This was 'Greenbank', the home of James Bythell ('Bethell' in the Tithe Apportionment), an elderly farmer, and his wife Jane. James rented the house from William Renshaw, who also owned one of the cottages at the end of the track. In the same house as James Bythell lived Jeremiah Renshaw, William's brother. He was the first of the many doctors in the area named Renshaw. 30 years old, he lived with his wife Maria, their small child and one servant. He was the father of Charles and the uncle of Israel Renshaw, both of whom became doctors and wrote books on aspects of the history of Ashton-upon-Mersey. As already mentioned, in the Tithe Apportionment we find him living in a newly-built house across the road in Ashton. Further down towards the canal were three small rented cottages, the homes of William Royle (agricultural worker), Joseph Burgess (farmer, 8 acres) and Peter Royle (agricultural worker) with their families.

On the north corner of Roebuck Lane and Washway Road was 'Sale Bank', described in one of the directories of the time as a 'neat stuccoed Gothic residence'. It stood in its own grounds, surrounded by trees. It had been built two or three years earlier for Samuel Roebuck, after whom the road was eventually named. Samuel lived at Sale Bank with his wife Hannah, their two children and five servants. Born in Salford in 1797, he had married the daughter of William Richardson, a grocer. Soon he was made a partner and the firm became Richardson and Roebuck, retail and wholesale grocers with two premises in Manchester (Market Place and Deansgate). They had a warrant to supply groceries to Queen Victoria. Also living in the house in 1841 was 60-year old William Richardson, Samuel's partner and father-in-law. Between Roebuck Lane and School Road were fields, with one house just south of the end of modern Sibson Road and another right at the junction with School Road. The first (named 'Roadside' in the census) was the home of Thomas Royle, a 62-year old gardener, who owned the house and four fields next to the house. Thomas was a widower, living with his son James and a housekeeper. Just before the corner of Washway Road and School Road was the house rented by Thomas Gardiner, a hatter, aged 31 and born in Warwickshire. In addition to his wife Anne and three children, he had a journeyman hatter and an apprentice living with him. Also in the house were three other families, including Jane Malley, a 15-year old schoolmistress.

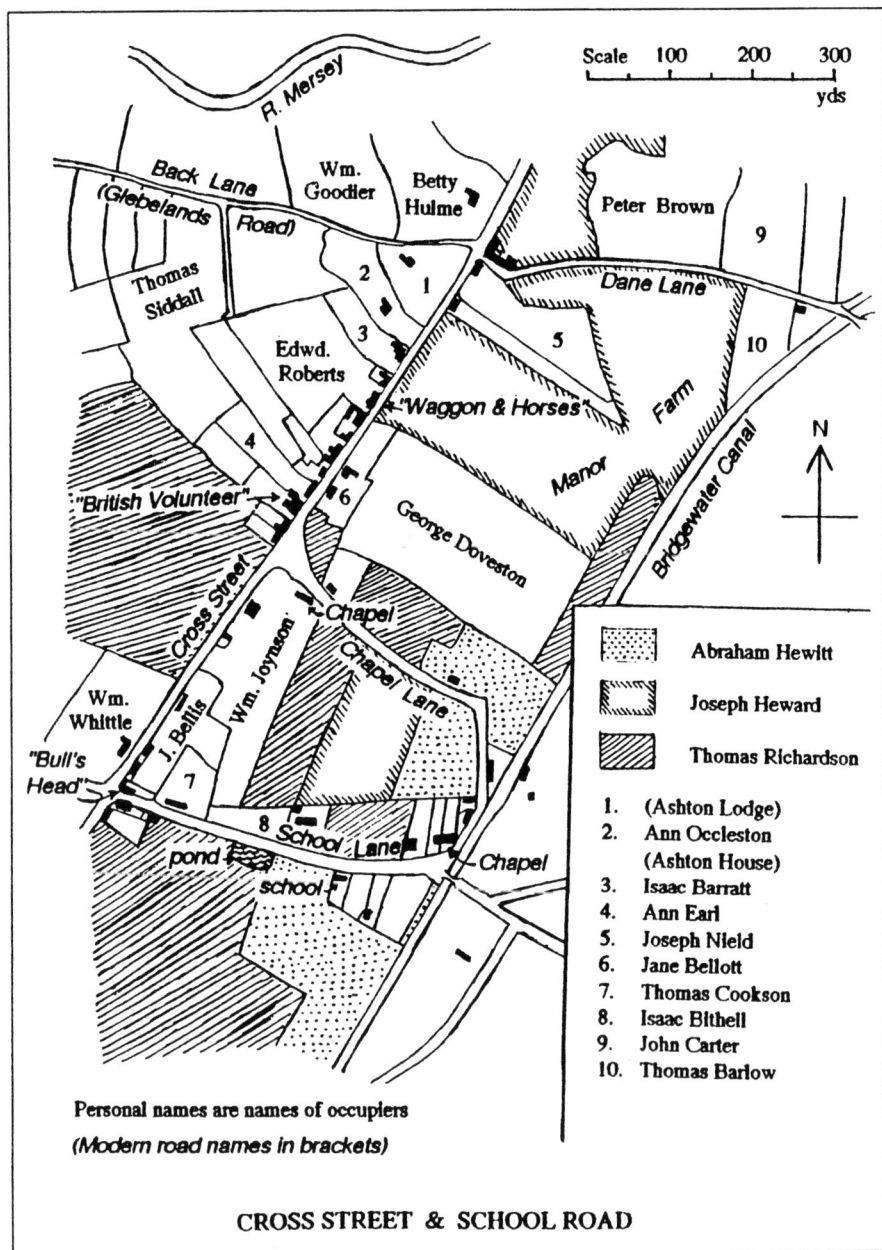

Scale 100 200 300
yds

R. Mersey

Back Lane
(Glebelands Road)

Wm. Goodier

Betty Hulme

Peter Brown

9

Thomas Siddall

2

1

Dane Lane

Edwd. Roberts

3

5

10

"Waggon & Horses"

Manor Farm

Bridgewater Canal

N

4

"British Volunteer"

6

George Doveston

Cross Street

Chapel

Wm. Joynson

Chapel Lane

Wm. Whittle

J. Bellis

"Bull's Head"

7

Abraham Hewitt

Joseph Heward

Thomas Richardson

8 School Lane

Chapel

pond

school

1. (Ashton Lodge)
2. Ann Occleston
   (Ashton House)
3. Isaac Barratt
4. Ann Earl
5. Joseph Nield
6. Jane Bellott
7. Thomas Cookson
8. Isaac Bithell
9. John Carter
10. Thomas Barlow

Personal names are names of occupiers

(Modern road names in brackets)

CROSS STREET & SCHOOL ROAD

26

3. Cross Street

The half-mile section of the A56 between School Road and the River Mersey is 'Cross Street'. It ends at the bridge carrying the road over the River Mersey. This is 'Crossford Bridge', a name which gives a clue to the past. It seems that before the river was bridged at this point, there was a ford marked by a cross. 'Cross Street' would therefore be the road leading to the cross; if this is true, the name goes back to the period before a bridge was built in mediaeval times. Because of the buildings built on either side of the road, in 1841 Cross Street was much narrower than Washway Road.

Although the original settlements of Ashton and Sale were well away from the main road, by the time of the seventeenth and eighteenth centuries traffic along the road had increased, and a number of houses were built on the roadside, especially on the Ashton side. The resulting hamlet was called 'Cross Street' and it is interesting to see that early county directories list Ashton-upon-Mersey and Cross Street, but do not mention Sale.

Walking down the west side of the road from Ashton Lane we would see a number of fields and then a row of houses starting opposite the end of Chapel Road. In the fields there was one building – the smithy of William Whittle. He was 50-years old and lived with his eight children, another man (possibly his brother) and one servant. Presumably he enjoyed a good trade from the many vehicles passing up and down the road. In addition to the smithy William owned a garden and three fields next to it and also rented two fields on Glebelands Road. Whittle Street was named after him, but was demolished in 1982 to make way for the new law courts. Between the smithy and the first house was an extremely large field called 'Park Field'. This belonged to Thomas Atkinson, whose name is perpetuated in Atkinson Road, which was later built down the middle of the field. Thomas Atkinson owned much of the land between Sibson Road and Chapel Road, and most of his land was rented to Thomas Richardson (see below).

There were seventeen houses between the large field and Glebelands Road. Some of them had gardens behind, others had yards enclosed by walls. It is not easy to decide exactly who lived in every house because of the difficulties already mentioned in the 'Introduction'. The first two houses were the homes of Robert Williamson (an elderly silk weaver) and Ellen Hartley, a 70-year old lady who took in lodgers. Then came the 'British Volunteer' public house, built around 1800 as the 'White Lion'. It was kept by Richard Simcoe, aged 20, who had taken it over from his father on the latter's death six months previously. The rest of Richard's household consisted of his wife, Drusilla, his young sister and a servant. Next were two more houses, the homes of a draper, a farmer, and a tailor, with their families and servants. The tailor, Thomas Hewitt, aged 40, had two apprentices. Then came a house which contained two fustian cutters, an agricultural labourer, a washerwoman and two brickmakers – with their families, a total of 18 people. George Doveston rented the next house from John Moore. George was a cabinet-maker, aged 40, and his household consisted of his wife, Hester, one daughter, his mother-in-law, and one 15-year old servant girl. George also rented a large garden behind his house and 2 fields across the road. His name is perpetuated in Doveston Road. Next door to the Dovestons were four houses, the homes of 35 people with a variety of jobs and trades. There was a joiner, a small-ware dealer, a shoemaker, a general agent, and several agricultural labourers. The shoemaker, who came from Ireland, had a servant living with him.

'The Waggon and Horses' public house was the next building. This had been built in 1788 and was now kept by 69-year old Edward Roberts, who also rented the large garden behind. He was assisted by his wife, Elizabeth, plus a brewer, and two servants. After the inn came the house of Peter Hesketh, a grocer. He was 59 years old, and lived with his wife, Martha, and two grown-up children. A little nearer to Glebelands Road was the house of Isaac Barrett. He was a saddler, aged 50, born in Hale, and now living in Ashton with his wife, Alice, and two children. Isaac owned four other houses in Ashton, plus the large garden behind his Cross Street house. He also leased nine houses in the neighbouring parish of Carrington. By the time of the 1851 census he had become a 'yeoman'. There were two other houses before Glebelands Road was reached. The first of these ('Ashton House') was set back from the main road, in a very large garden which reached right through to Glebelands Road. This was the home of Ann Occleston, a widow aged 60 with five children. She had independent means and employed two servants to look after the house and family. The second house ('Ashton Lodge') was also owned by the Occlestons; it was situated nearer to Glebelands Road, but was approached by a drive leading from Cross Street. We do not know for certain who lived in this house in 1841; it appears to have been Henry Hughes, a horse dealer. Born in Ireland, he was 52 years of age, and lived with his wife Mary, and one son. An agricultural labourer also lived with them. In June 1842 the house was sold to John Gallemore, a calico printer, who later moved out from Manchester. He died in February, 1848.

There were two buildings between Glebelands Road and the township/county boundary. The first, 'Elmfield', was a large house set back from the road, and surrounded by a large garden. Here lived Betty Hulme, with her three grown-up daughters and two servants. Betty was a widow in her seventies, and she also owned 'Chapel Field', next door to the house. This was the site of the first non-conformist chapel in Ashton and Sale, built by the Presbyterians around 1695, soon after the passing of the Toleration Act of 1689, which allowed freedom of worship to everyone except Unitarians. The chapel was closed in 1739 and finally pulled down in 1805, when many of the stones were used to line the cellars of the neighbouring buildings in Cross Street. As mentioned on p.2, here at Crossford Bridge the River Mersey did not form the boundary between Lancashire and Cheshire; the actual boundary was 75 yards south of the bridge. Just inside the Ashton boundary was the Toll Bar, where vehicles had to stop to pay for their passage through the township. This had been built when the road was turnpiked in 1765. The toll-bar keeper was 48-year old George Blackman, who lived in the toll house with his wife, Mary.

We now retrace our steps to School Road and look at the Sale side of Cross Street. At the corner of School Road and Cross Street stood the 'Bull's Head', as it does today; the 1841 building, however, was much smaller, and had one storey only. The licensee was Peter Tyrer. As was usual at the time, he had a second occupation – he was also a butcher, a trade he had learned from his father who lived at the other end of Sale. Aged 33, he lived with his wife, Elizabeth, and their five young children. The bull's head was part of the crest of the Massey family, the first 'lords of the manor' of Sale. Another 20 people seem to have been living in the 'Bull's Head' at the time of the census. One of these was a merchant from Scotland, with his wife, six children and four servants. Peter Tyrer was one of the Township Assessors of Assessed Taxes in 1841. There was a white cottage next to the inn – the home of Richard Bancroft, a fustian cutter. Richard was 35, and lived with his wife, two apprentices, and another lady, possibly his mother-in-law.

Next to this was a second white cottage, where a joiner, Joseph Moores, lived with his family. Another lady and a fustian cutter seem to have been lodgers. Further along the road there was a house which was unoccupied at the time of the census; it was the home of John Bellis when the Tithe Apportionment was drawn up. Much of the land between School Road and Chapel Road was owned by Thomas Atkinson. In the middle of it was a house rented by John Hulbert, a man of independent means in his fifties, living with his wife, Betty. John was obviously a man of some standing, as he was one of the enumerators for the 1841 census and he also owned two other houses, one of them being that of Joseph Moores above.

On the south corner of Cross Street and Chapel Road was a plot of land rented by the Unitarians. The large house on the main road seems to have been empty in 1841, but a few years later it was occupied by a solicitor and silk manufacturer, William Joynson, who became the first Chairman of the newly-formed Sale Urban District Council in 1867. His name and that of his house ('Ashfield House') are commemorated by street names. On the opposite corner was the farm of 51-years old Thomas Richardson, who rented his farmhouse and fifteen fields from Thomas Atkinson. These fields covered 54 acres, stretching from the modern Sibson Road to the north side of Chapel Road. In addition, Thomas rented a further 32 acres across the road in Ashton. Thomas's wife, Elizabeth, and five children lived with him. They had two servants to help with the house and the farm. Next to the farmhouse was a large rectangular block of land reaching almost to the canal. This belonged to John Moore. On the roadside there were two buildings; one of which remains today as the oldest building in Sale. In 1841 they were both rented by Jane Bellott ('Bellard' in the Tithe Apportionment), who ran a private school for 'young ladies'. Jane was 65 and had her daughter (also a schoolmistress) and another elderly schoolteacher living with her. They had one servant to help them. The house, now known as 'Eyebrow Cottage', was built towards the end of the seventeenth century. It was owned by Captain John Moore, who had lived in it for some years as 'Lord of the Manor' before it was rented to Miss Bellott. The house was therefore known as 'the Old Manor House', according to correspondence in the 'Manchester City News' in 1895, and appears as such in late nineteenth-century directories.

Near the junction with Dane Road were two houses. The first was the home of Mary Alcock, a widow, living with her two grown-up sons, who were agricultural labourers. At the junction itself was the home of Joseph Nield, a joiner, aged 51. He was the Churchwarden appointed for Sale Old Hall, and lived with his wife, Hannah, five children and three servants. Dane Road narrowed considerably at its junction with Cross Street. On the north side of the junction was Manor Farm (the name and location support the view that the 'Manor House' was at one time the building on Cross Street and not Sale Old Hall). The main building of the farm was L-shaped, facing on to both Cross Street and Dane Road. The farm was the property of the executors of Peter Heward and covered a large area, including two fields at the back of Roebuck Lane, one field of Chapel Road, and a number of fields on both sides of Dane Road. In 1841 it was occupied by two of Peter's sons, Thomas and Joseph. Thomas was a farmer and Joseph was a licensed brewer; both of them were bachelors. They had two servants living in. By 1844 Thomas had died and Joseph was now listed as a 'beer-retailer'. The census lists the names of 33 other people who appear to have lived at or near the farm. They included a ropemaker, a wheelwright, a slater, a police constable (John Topham), a shoemaker, all with their respective families. Manor Farm was not finally demolished until around 1950.

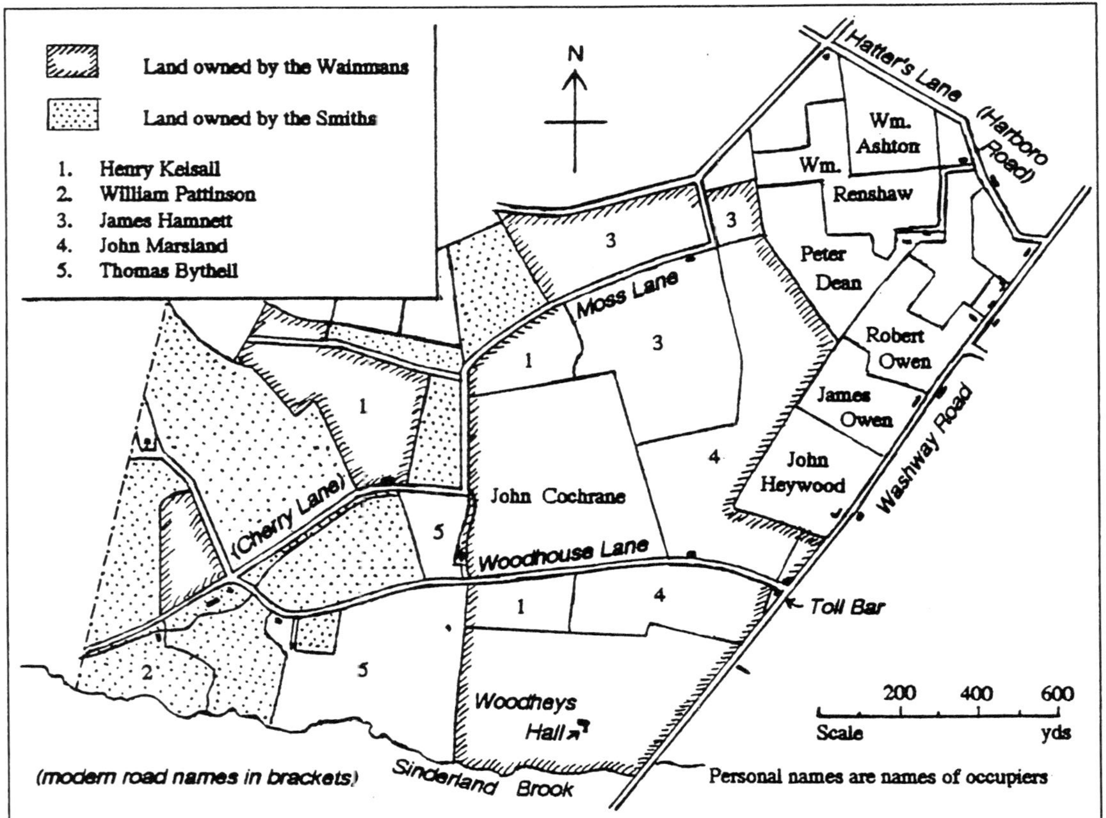
Land owned by the Wainmans
Land owned by the Smiths
1. Henry Kelsall
2. William Pattinson
3. James Hamnett
4. John Marsland
5. Thomas Bythell
N
Hatter's Lane
(Harboro Road)
Wm. Ashton
Wm. Renshaw
Peter Dean
Robert Owen
James Owen
John Heywood
Washway Road
Moss Lane
John Cochrane
Woodhouse Lane
(Cherry Lane)
Toll Bar
Woodheys Hall
Sinderland Brook
200
400
600
Scale
yds
(modern road names in brackets)
Personal names are names of occupiers

MOSS LANE & ASHTON WOODHOUSES

4. Woodhouse Lane and Moss Lane

Woodhouse Lane ran westwards from the Washway Toll House to the Carrington boundary. It follows the same route today, although in 1841 it was no more than a cart track. It led to 'Ashton Woodhouses', which was a cluster of three or four farms separated from Ashton and Sale by fields until the 1930's. From Ashton Woodhouses it was possible to see over the fields to St. Martin's Church at the other end of the township, especially in winter when the trees had shed their leaves.

Most of the land between Sinderland Brook and Moss Lane was owned in 1841 by two families – the Wainmans (of Woodheys Hall) and the Smiths – and was rented out to tenant farmers. The first farm along Woodhouse Lane was that of John Marsland. The farm buildings stood at the corner where Meadway would later join; the farm lands, rented from Major Wainman, lay on both sides of Woodhouse Lane and stretched right up to Moss Lane. John Marsland lived with his wife, Elizabeth, their seven children (eldest one aged 11) and two servants. The second farm was at the bottom of the modern Manor Avenue. This also belonged to Major Wainman and was run by John Cochrane, who lived with his wife, Jane, and one servant. There was another farm on the south side of Woodhouse Lane, where it bends north-westwards to join Cherry Lane. The farmhouse ('Woodhouse Farm') is still in existence today, having been attractively restored as a private house. In 1841 it belonged neither to the Wainmans nor the Smiths, but to the Earl of Stamford. The tenant farmer was Thomas Bythell, who was a widower (his wife had died 6 months previously) living with two teenage children and five servants (two of the latter being aged 10!). Except for one field on the opposite side, his farm lands lay between Woodhouse Lane and Sinderland Brook. Also living with them were two agricultural labourers and James Lawton Richardson, an auctioneer, with his family. James owned four houses in Ashton village; these were rented out to various tenants. At the junction of Woodhouse Lane and Cherry Lane was the home of Ann Smith, an 81-year-old widow of independent means. Next to her house was the farmstead where her son, Charles lived with his wife, Ann, and nine servants. The Smiths had farmed there for over a hundred years, and their lands were quite extensive, stretching from Sinderland Brook right up into the modern 'Racecourse' estate. Charles also owned 73 acres of land across the parish boundary in Carrington. The farm had been built in 1697. Right at the end of Woodhouse Lane, near the Carrington boundary, was another farm ('Brook Cottage'), which was rented from the Smiths by William Pattinson. He lived with his wife, Ann, and two people of independent means (one probably being his mother-in-law). All four of them came from outside Cheshire. The stream which gave the farm its name ran along the south side of Cherry Lane and right through the gardens of the last three properties, flowing through two ponds in Pattinson's farm to join Sinderland Brook just over the Carrington boundary.

Opposite the junction of Woodhouse Lane and Cherry Lane a short path ran to the north-west, roughly on the line of the modern Firs Way. At the end of the path were the house and garden of Ann Holt, a widow who lived with her two sons (agricultural labourers). It seems that the house (one of several in Ashton named 'Moss Cottage') was at one time in Carrington parish, if the accuracy of old pre-Ordnance Survey maps is to be trusted. The house has been much enlarged but survives today with boarding kennels attached.

There was track which ran along the line of the modern Cherry Lane, turning left into Manor Avenue and then right into the modern Moss Lane. Along Cherry Lane was Gnat Hall (later, 'Knathall') Farm, which was built around 1800 on the site of the former Gnat Hall, the home of Dr. Peter Mainwaring. The site is now where Hurst Avenue meets Cherry Lane. This farm also belonged to Major Wainman, and in 1841 the tenant farmer was 29-year-old Henry Kelsall, who had a wife, Rachel, three small children and three servants. Turning into Moss Lane, we would find a farm near the junction with the modern Cecil Avenue. This was rented from Major Wainman by a 'James Hamnett', but as there were three men of this name in the vicinity, we do not know which one. The census does not help us and the farm had disappeared by 1876. At the junction with the modern Moss Way the track crossed over Button Brook. Further on, at the corner of Moss Lane and Harboro Road was the house and garden of Rachel Irlam. She was 82 years old, a widow, and lived with her son William, a farmer, and his four children. Rachel died in 1843 and the lease of the property was transferred not to her son William but to a John Renshaw (presumably a relative).

5. Harboro Road and Firs Road

Harboro Road

Harboro Road received its modern name sometime before 1876. In 1841, however, the section between Washway Road and Moss Lane was called 'Hatters' Lane', and the section between Moss Lane and Firs Road was 'Jacksmith Lane'. The origin of these names is not known.

Walking from Washway Road, we would find the first house on the east side of the road. This was the home of William Brundrett, a 45-year-old gardener, his wife, Hannah, and their four children. William owned a field next to the house, and the site later became a nursery. William also received extra income from Ivy Farm in Firs Road, which he owned and rented to Thomas Jones. William's name is perpetuated in 'Brundrett Place', which was built on the site of his house in 1989. A little further up, a track on the opposite side of the road led to Woodheys Nook. For a short distance the track ran alongside a stream (Button Brook) and a bridge over the stream led to Woodheys Nook Farm (later 'Woodheys Farm'), owned by Peter Dean. He was 53 years old, and had a wife and six children. The thatched, whitewashed farm buildings, which were situated on the site of the modern 35-39 Cecil Avenue, were demolished in 1950. The farm lands consisted of six fields to the west of the farmhouse, and had been the property of the Dean family for over 60 years. Peter also owned the house next door, which he rented to Joseph Harrop, one of his labourers. Joseph and his wife had five children. In addition to these properties, Peter owned a cottage on the edge of the Moss. Returning to Harboro Road, there was a small row of houses belonging to the Cross Street Chapel trustees. These were the homes of William Goodier, a farmer, and two other families, in both of which the husband was named 'James Davenport'; presumably they were father and son. They were both 'hot-platers' by trade; the elder James (aged 55) died six months after the census was taken. Martha, the wife of the younger one is interesting because she was born in France.

Proceeding further, past Rachel Irlam's house at the corner of Moss Lane, we would come to another 'Moss Cottage'. This was the home of

Newton Green (see p.40). (Photograph by the author.)

George Derbyshire. Although he stated that he was a 'farmer' in the census, he in fact rented only two fields. He lived with his wife, Alice, and their five children. The cottage is now a listed building. 200 yards further along was Weathercock Farm, which survived until the site was made into a recreation ground in the 1960's. Weathercock Farm was rented by James Hamnett, who was 52. He lived with his wife, Alice, their two teenage children and five servants. The farm lands consisted of seven fields round the house, plus three over by the River Mersey.

Firs Road

Until 1890 there were two 'Moss Lanes', both leading out on to Carrington Moss. Around 1890 the most northerly one became 'Moss Lane West', a name it retained until 1924, when it was re-named 'Firs Road', because it led to Firs Farm. The latter was situated at the edge of the Moss, near a plantation of fir trees, some of which are still standing along the side of Firs Way.

At the corner of Harboro Road and Firs Road was the house of James Derbyshire. He lived with his family (his wife and five children), with his son and his family (his wife and very small daughter), plus another family (husband, wife and two children). All the men were agricultural labourers. A little further down Firs Road, on the opposite side, was the house of Charles Tonge, a gardener. Charles was 26 and he and his wife Mary had four children (the oldest being 4 years old), and one servant. There were two farms along Firs Road. The first was Fiddler's Green Farm, later called 'Oaklee Farm'. The farm buildings were set back from the road, standing on the site of the modern Okehampton Crescent. The farm was rented by Samuel Davenport, who was 54 years old, and lived with his wife, Sarah, one son, and five servants. On the other side of the road was Ivy Farm, which was rented by Thomas Jones from William Brundrett. Thomas rented a number of fields from Brundrett and also from two other people. He lived with his wife, Margaret, their two daughters and five servants. Further west, in the area of the modern Gaydon Road, the path divided into three. The right-hand track led to a small house alongside Button Brook. This seems to have been the home of Thomas Higson, gamekeeper. The central track of the three crossed over Button Brook and led first to Moss Farm, which belonged to Major Wainman. It was rented by Thomas Bancroft, who lived there with his wife, Mary and six children. According to the census, all six were 'servants'; in addition, there were two other servants. The farm buildings were situated off Firs Way, where Firtree Avenue is today. On the other side of the road was the house and garden belonging to Martha Jones, a 60-year-old lady of independent means. Also living in the house were her son, William, and his family (wife and six children) and one servant. Martha owned a number of fields in the vicinity. The third of the tracks crossed over Button Brook and led out on to the Moss.

6. Barkers Lane and Ashton Lane

Barkers Lane

Both Barkers Lane and Ashton Lane followed their present course in 1841. 'Barkers Lane' took its name from Richard Robinson, alias 'Richard Barker', a member of the family who owned the land on both sides of the lane around the beginning of the nineteenth century. Along the whole length of Barkers Lane there were only four houses. The first house, on the bend, was the home of Edward Dean, a 52-year old nurseryman, whose wife, Ellen, came from Wales; they had five children below the age of 10. Further up were two houses, one on each side of the road. In the one on the left lived three families, those of John Singleton, John Dunn (agricultural labourers) and John Bennett (carrier). Between them they had fifteen children. On the other side of the lane was the farm rented by James Renshaw. He was 55 years old and lived with his wife, Jane, and one servant. The seven farm fields were scattered all over Ashton and included one on the north side of the River Mersey. Next door to the farm was the cottage of William Holliday, a coachman, aged 24, living with his wife and two small children.

Ashton Lane

Except for the Wesleyan Methodist Chapel on the main road and the row of five houses next to it, the whole of the triangle enclosed by Barkers Lane, Washway Road and Ashton Lane contained nothing but fields. The first house in Ashton Lane was that of the elderly James Woodall. He was 72, a (retired?) agricultural labourer, living with an 86-year-old lady. On the first bend there were two houses, one on each side. On the left lived John Whitelegg, a farmer, living with his wife, Hannah, their four small children and five servants. Nearly opposite the Whiteleggs was a field where 'Whitefield House' would be built around 1845. This was built for John Earle Gallemore, a calico printer who moved from Stretford to live in Sale (John Gallemore, his father, later moved to 'Ashton Lodge' on Cross Street). John the son died in December, 1851. His house (now 'The Old Coach House') and the lodge are still there on Ashton Lane. Almost next door was 'Oak Villa', the home of John Andrews, an attorney with chambers in Back King Street, Manchester. His wife, Ann, their two small children and four servants lived with him. John died in 1844 at the age of 38. Beyond 'Oak Villa' there were two more houses. The first was the home of Thomas Siddall, a 40-year-old farmer. He lived with his wife, Mary, their four children and four servants. His farm lands included two large fields on the south side of Moss Lane, a number of fields near the house and a few at the far end of the parish, near the River Mersey. At the junction of Barkers Lane and Ashton Lane was a grassy area named 'Newton Green'. The site is now marked by a flower-bed planted out by the Council each spring and a truncated pillar, which is all that remains of the drinking-fountain presented in 1881 by Sir William Cunliffe-Brooks. The 'Green' took its name from the Newton family who lived on the opposite side of the road. Their house, which became known as 'Newton Green Farm', was bought by the family in 1689 and in 1841 was the home of Robert Newton (a farmer, aged 72) and his wife, Hannah. Robert also owned thirteen fields, mostly near his house, which is still lived in today as a private house.

Further along towards Ashton village there were two houses with gardens, which were approached by a private road roughly on the line of the present Grosvenor Road. At the time of the Tithe Apportionment, they both were leased by William Ashton, Robert Newton's son-in-law. It seems probable that 1841 one was the home of Robert Newton (the younger). He was the son of the Robert at Newton Green next door, and lived with seven servants. Unfortunately he died in 1842 at the age of 33. The farmhouse was later known as 'Grange Farm'. The farm lands were extensive, with some fields at the far end of Moss Lane and others stretching as far as Dumber Lane. Slightly nearer Ashton village, on the opposite side of Ashton Lane, were two houses, known as 'Coffer Trap Cottages'. These were the home of four families; three were the families of agricultural workers, the fourth was an elderly 'pauper' with three children. One of the houses, 'Yew Bank Cottage', remains inhabited today. Rather confusingly it bears the date '1845', although 'Coffer Trap Cottages' are listed in the 1841 census. The other house was demolished in the 1960's to make way for a block of flats.

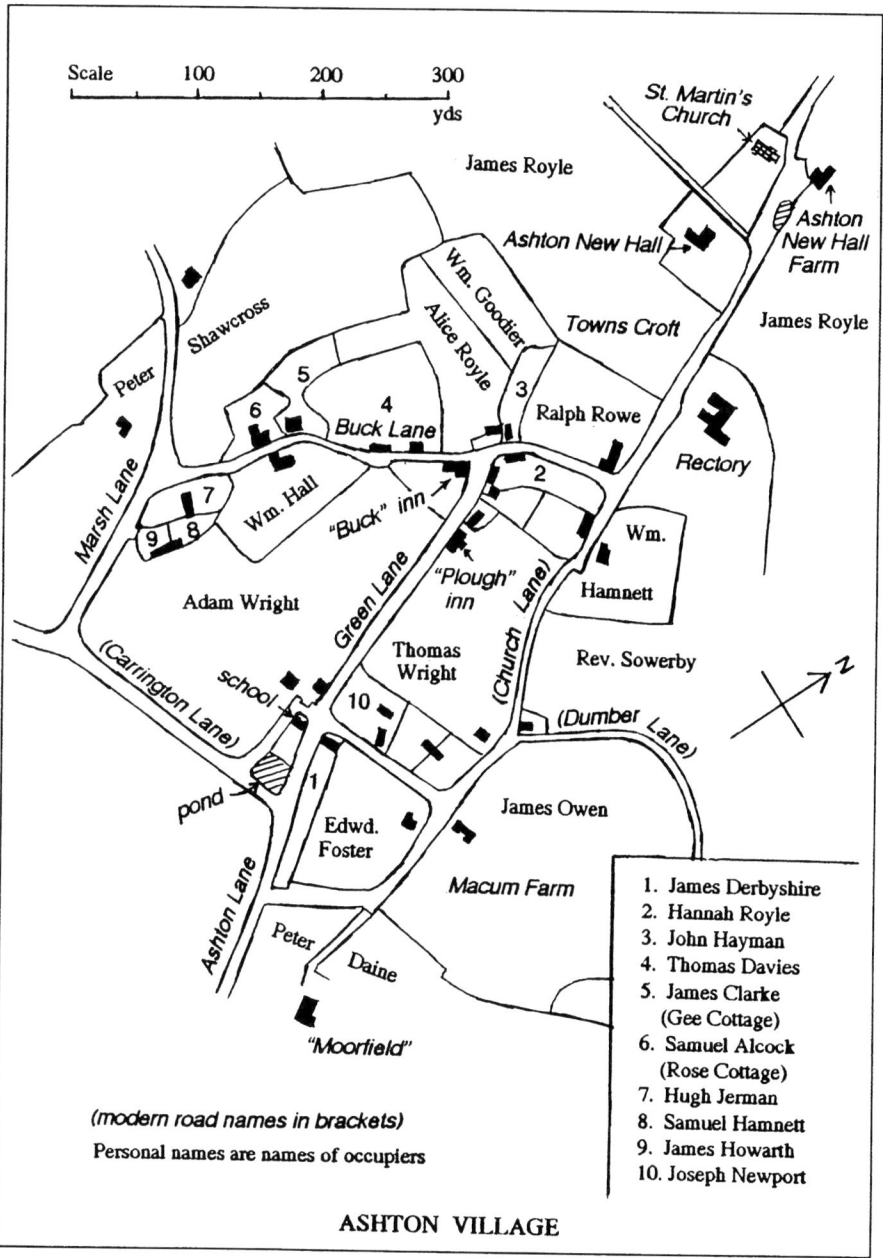

Scale 100 200 300
yds

St. Martin's Church

James Royle

Ashton New Hall

Ashton New Hall Farm

Wm. Goodier

Towns Croft

James Royle

Shawcross

Alice Royle

Peter

5

6

4

Buck Lane

3

Ralph Rowe

Marsh Lane

7

Wm. Hall

9   8

"Buck" inn

Green Lane

2

Rectory

Adam Wright

"Plough" inn

(Church Lane)

Wm. Hamnett

(Carrington Lane)

school

Thomas Wright

Rev. Sowerby

pond

10

(Dumber Lane)

1

James Owen

Ashton Lane

Edwd. Foster

Macum Farm

Peter Daine

"Moorfield"

(modern road names in brackets)

Personal names are names of occupiers

1. James Derbyshire
2. Hannah Royle
3. John Hayman
4. Thomas Davies
5. James Clarke
   (Gee Cottage)
6. Samuel Alcock
   (Rose Cottage)
7. Hugh Jerman
8. Samuel Hamnett
9. James Howarth
10. Joseph Newport

ASHTON VILLAGE

41

7. Ashton Village

The road layout of Ashton village in 1841 was very similar to that of today. Green Lane, Buck Lane, Chapel Lane and Church Lane were all there; the only roads missing were Greenbank Road, Buckfast Road and the stretch of Glebelands Road from Church Lane to the bottom of Dumber Lane. Other minor roads, of course, were not built until much later. The appearance of the village, however, was far different. Although there were over 35 houses, most of the 'village' area consisted of gardens and orchards, with the buildings scattered here and there (the one exception being the junction of Buck Lane and Green Lane, where there were a number of buildings). Ashton was, however, a 'real' village, with church, school, two public houses, and a number of shops and tradesmen, in sharp contrast to Sale, which was a large area of scattered farms and houses, devoid of any real centre. Ashton village represents the only 'old' corner of Sale and Ashton to be seen today, as approximately a third of the buildings are still standing.

The position of the ancient church – right on the northern edge of the village – has led to suggestions that the mediaeval village of 'Ashton-upon-Mersey Bank' (as it was at one time named) was located nearer the river. Field names certainly point to a water-mill having been situated on the river bank to the north of the church. The frequent floods caused by the Mersey overflowing were a constant source of trouble to villagers right up to the end of the nineteenth century and could have provided an adequate reason for moving the village away from the river.

Green Lane and Chapel Lane
Standing at the junction of Carrington Lane and Ashton Lane we would see on our left the township school, run by John Fletcher. It was replaced in 1874 by another school built by Sir William Cunliffe-Brooks on the same site. The old school was very small; in front of it was a garden, and in front of that, in Carrington Lane, was a large pond. In the census John Fletcher was described as an 'agent'. Born in Yorkshire in 1797, he had married a Sale girl; he and his wife Grace lodged with Elizabeth Royle. Three years later he and his wife had their own house in the village, with a schoolmistress (John's sister-in-law) as lodger. A path led round the back of the school to Carrington

Lane, a route still taken by pedestrians, who now have to walk through a car-park.

We do not know what Chapel Lane was called in 1841, or even whether it had a name at all. It became 'Chapel Lane' after the opening of the Primitive Methodist Chapel on the south side of the lane in May, 1853.

There were two houses on the site of the modern filling station. In the Tithe Apportionment these were rented by James Darbyshire from Ashton-on-Mersey Friendly Society. James was a 48-year old agricultural labourer, and the houses were occupied by a number of other labourers with their families. Local tradition says that the Pinfold (the place where stray animals were kept until claimed by their owners and any damage done paid for) was in Chapel Lane; there was also a large field called 'Pinfold Field' in Church Lane, on the site of the modern Wellfield Infants School. On the north side of Chapel Lane there were four houses with large gardens. One of the houses was the home of Joseph Newport, a bachelor of independent means. The other inhabitants of the houses appear to have been a lady of independent means, a tailor, a blacksmith, and some agricultural labourers, all with their families.

Green Lane is now the 'commercial centre' of Ashton village. There is a supermarket, a post office, and all the other buildings are either shops or offices. In 1841 there were gardens and fields on either side of Green Lane. On the left there were no buildings between the corner of Greenbank Road and the 'Buck' inn. The area between was an extensive garden which was rented by Adam Wright. He also rented the two houses which stood at what is now the corner of Greenbank Road. Adam was a farm labourer, and lived with his wife, two children and two lodgers. On the right hand side was a large field, over which it was possible to see the obelisk halfway down Dumber Lane. Beyond this one could see the trees along the River Mersey and even into Lancashire. At the junction of Green Lane and Buck Lane were several buildings. On the left corner was the 'Buck' inn, kept by Elizabeth Watson. She was 55 and had two sons living with her, plus a wheelwright (born in Ireland), two servants and three farm labourers. There was a wheelwright's shop in the yard, and, when Elizabeth died in 1842, we find that one of her sons, John, also a wheelwright, had taken over the inn. According to articles in the 'Sale Guardian' in 1958, the inn was where the Court Leet of Ashton met. The cellar on the right

Macum Cottage (see p.46). (Photograph by the author.)

hand side of the entrance had been used as a prison, and there was a treadmill in another cellar. Many people believe that Buck Lane goes right down to meet Church Lane; in fact, the section between the 'Buck' inn and Church Lane is part of Green Lane. Along this portion were several houses. The first three were occupied by William Goodier and John Hayman (agricultural labourers), and Alice Royle. The last-named was 70 years old and described herself as a 'farmer'. She had three daughters and a servant living with her. She owned the house, three fields behind the house and one other on the banks of the River Mersey. John Hayman's house remains as a DIY and garden shop. The last house was near the junction with Church Lane. This was the home of Ralph Rowe (Wroe), a market gardener aged 34, living with his wife and two children. The house was on the site of the 'Towns Croft' Residential Home ('Towns Croft' was the name of a large field between Ralph Rowe's house and Ashton New Hall).

On the other side of Green Lane there were four buildings, all at the north end; the first of them was the 'Plough' inn (now the 'Old Plough'). In the Tithe Apportionment the building was leased to Thomas Wright, a farmer (see below). The actual inn-keeper in 1841, however, was 32-year old John Aldcroft. His household consisted of his wife, Martha, three children and two servants. The inn was well-known as the location where Captain John Moore first raised his 'Ashton-upon-Mersey Volunteers' in 1803. Two of the other buildings were the homes of John Cook and Hannah Royle. John was a joiner and shop-keeper, aged 50. He owned his house, and lived with his wife, Sarah, and a servant. One of the houses still carries a plaque with the date '1809'.

Church Lane

In 1841 Church Lane had three names. The western part was 'Dean's Lane', named after the Daine family (see below). The middle section between Chapel Lane and Green Lane was 'Macum Lane', a name probably originating from Roger Macome, who had a farm in Ashton (Macum Farm?) in 1628. The northern portion was 'Church Lane', and about 1880 this name was applied to all three sections.

If we were to return to the junction of Ashton Lane and Church Lane, and walk down the latter, the first house we would see would be 'Moorfield', with its drive starting at the bend by the 'Pinfold Field'. The house and the area round it had belonged to the Daine family for over 150 years. In 1841 it was the home of Peter Daine, a 60-year-old man of independent means. He had a wife, Jane, three children, and one servant. 'Moorfield' was demolished in 1956 to make way for the houses on Monmouth Avenue. Further along the lane, opposite the end of Chapel Lane, stood Macum Farm. In 1841 it was rented by James Owen, whose farm covered 29 fields in several parts of Ashton. Some of the fields were behind the farm buildings, but most of them were along Glebelands Road. James was 44, and his household consisted of his wife, Mary, their seven children and two servants. Macum Farm was demolished in 1973 to make way for modern housing and the school. Edward Foster lived in the house opposite. He was 43 and a market gardener, born in Ireland. He lived with his wife, Martha, two small children and two servants (also born in Ireland). At the junction of Church Lane and Dumber Lane we would see a small cottage ('Macum Cottage'), which is still there. In 1841 it was the home of Betty Royle, who took in lodgers. On the other side of the road lived Thomas Wright, a farmer aged 46. He had a wife, Jane, five children, and three agricultural labourers living with him. He rented the 'Plough' inn, the field next to it, and also five fields off Harboro Road. Nearer to the end of Green Lane was a house which survives as 'The Coach House'. This was rented by William Hamnett, an agricultural labourer aged 44, with a wife and six children. He also rented the two old thatched cottages which faced them.

Church Lane continued down towards the church, with the rectory on the east side, and Ashton New Hall on the west. The rectory was set back from the lane, in an extensive garden. The house was large, as befitted one of the most important men in the community. The rector of Ashton from 1835 to 1866 was the Rev. Charles Sowerby. Born in Hertfordshire, he was educated at University College, Oxford. In 1841 he was 45, living with his wife, Abigail, their children and three servants. His wife and children were away from home at the time of the census. In the grounds of the rectory there was an old yew tree, planted to commemorate the accession of Queen Elizabeth I in 1558. The rectory was demolished in 1915-6 and the land was sold for housing in 1925. The Rev. Sowerby was assisted by his curate, the Rev. John Hunter, who lived at Ashton New Hall, an attractive Georgian house built in 1804. John had married Sarah Stelfox, the heiress to the Williamson estate. The Williamsons had lived in Ashton since the time of James I, and their property included the Hall and the farm across the road. Two of Sarah's brothers had been killed at the Battle of Waterloo.

Born in Eccles, John Hunter was three years older than Charles Sowerby. In addition to being the curate at St. Martin's for 41 years from 1815 to 1856, he was schoolmaster in the Sale Township School for 18 years before the appointment of James Warren in 1836. Next to the New Hall (which is still lived in today) was the Church of St. Martin. The first church was originally built around 1300, possibly on the site of an earlier Saxon chapel. A new church had been built in 1714, with a clock tower donated by Joshua Renshaw. In 1841 the parishioners were getting used to the new organ, which had been recently installed to provide the music for services instead of the old church band (flute, bassoon, violins, cello). In the church yard there were several commemorative trees; these included an ash to mark the re-building and opening of the church in 1714 and a beech to commemorate the Battle of Waterloo. Outside the church was the mounting stone, where members of the congregation who came to church by horse could re-mount at the end of the service. Opposite the church stood Ashton Hall Farm, which was rented from the Rev. Hunter by James Royle. Because the farm belonged to the owner of Ashton New Hall, at some periods the farm has been known as 'Ashton New Hall Farm'; according to mid-nineteenth-century maps and directories, it was 'Ashton Old Hall', being the original hall before the New Hall was built. However, Lionel Angus-Butterworth (who lived in the New Hall for over thirty years) states that the New Hall was actually built on the site of the Old Hall, and the farm has always been only a farm. James Royle was 51, and lived with his wife, Mary, their seven children, his 85-year father and two servants. The main part of the farm lands were round the farm house itself, reaching right to the River Mersey. James also rented several fields from other people, and two of these were on the 'Moss', against the Carrington boundary. These James rented from his father, who presumably acquired them when part of the Moss was enclosed.

Buck Lane

On the north side of Buck Lane there were five houses, of which two are still standing today. The first two houses were owned by Thomas Davies, aged 38. His family had farmed in Ashton for two hundred years. The third ('Gee Cottage') was the home of James Clarke (shopkeeper and provision dealer), who was 43 and lived with his wife, two children and a lodger (a shoemaker). Gee Cottage is reputed to have been the old 'Manor House' of Ashton. It was built around 1712 and

Buck Lane, taken around 1900. (Photograph reproduced here by courtesy of Peter Hall.)

presumably took its name from the Gee family (who lived in Ashton between 1670 and 1750). 'Rose Cottage' and the house next door were rented by Samuel Alcock (agricultural labourer). He was 35 and his family consisted of his wife and three children. Opposite Samuel Alcock's houses was 'Daisy Cottage', the house of William Hall. He was a tailor, aged 74, living with his wife, Lucy, two grown-up children and a servant. His name is remembered in 'Hall Avenue', which is situated where his house stood. Another son, also named William, was a tailor at the other end of Sale. Right at the junction of Buck Lane and Carrington Lane were three houses which were rented by Hugh Jerman, Samuel Hamnett and James Howarth, all agricultural labourers with families. Samuel Hamnett had a servant to help look after him and his family.

8. Carrington Lane

The section of Carrington Lane between the end of Ashton Lane and Firs Road seems to have been called 'School Lane' until about 1900. The rest of Carrington Lane was 'Marsh Lane' until about the same date. This refers to the state of the ground, which was regularly flooded by the River Mersey. In fact, the names of six fields on the south side of the road referred to the marsh – three were named simply 'Marsh', and the other three were named 'Black Marsh', 'Great Marsh' and 'Near and Far Marsh'. Harboro Road finished at Firs Road in 1841 and the short straight section joining it to Carrington Lane at the top of Greenbank Road was not made until much later.

The first buildings along Carrington Lane were opposite the end of Buck Lane. These were the buildings of Royle Gate Farm (later 'White Gate Farm'), a 40-acre farm which Peter Shawcross leased from the Earl of Stamford. Peter was 45 and lived with two children and two servants. Nearer Carrington, on the opposite side of the road, was Marsh Farm, which today stands in the middle of modern housing. This was owned by John Davies, who lived with his wife, Ann, three small children and one servant. John was parish clerk and sexton. His farm lands were scattered – two fields near the farmhouse, four fields on the east side of Harboro Road and two fields on the north side of the modern Spur road. The next building poses something of a puzzle. It was named 'Barracks' and was situated where Brayton Avenue is today, in the middle of what was the 'Marsh'. At that time there were buildings named 'Barracks' in both Ashton and Sale. It seems that this word originally meant 'temporary buildings' before its usage was restricted to military establishments. This would explain the presence of 'Barracks' where no soldiers have been known. The barracks seem to have consisted of a number of houses, containing six agricultural labourers (with their families), one weaver (and his family) and Ann Legh, a lady of independent means, with her daughter, son, and grand-daughter. The property was rented by Samuel Davenport (who lived at Fiddler's Green Farm) and was sub-let to the inhabitants.

At the end of Barracks Lane was the small rented house of Samuel Kelsall. Samuel was a gardener aged 61, living with his wife, Margaret, and their seven children. They had a lady with two sons living with them, possibly relations. Down Barracks Lane was Barracks Farm, which still survives on the edge of the new housing development behind All Saints Church. A stone over the door says that the farm was built in 1714. It was rented and farmed by John Kelsall, a man aged 59. John's wife, Elizabeth, and their two sons lived with him, and also five servants. Four other people aged from 9 to 22 lived at the farm; their status is not known. Possibly they were relations, as nine servants would seem excessive. The two Kelsalls, Samuel and John, were probably related, possibly brothers, but their properties were rented from different owners. A later resident of Barracks Farm wrote that his father had to keep a boat on the farm because it was often cut off by floods (*Sale Guardian*, March 1958).

The last two farms faced each other, one on each side of the road not far from the township boundary. Both were owned by 27-year old John Newton, who lived in Mersey Farm with his wife, Harriet, their two small children and three servants. John's father was Robert Newton, who lived on Ashton Lane. Across the road was the farm which John Newton rented out to James Sherlock. The latter was 42 and lived with his wife and a servant. Three other people lived in the house; the census does not state whether they are relations or servants. James also rented ten fields round the farmhouse and one on the other side of the road. Eight of these were rented from John Newton and the others from another person.

Marsh Farm (see p.50). (Photograph by the author.)

52

9. Glebelands Road and Dumber Lane

Until about 1870 Glebelands Road was called 'Back Lane'. There is a tradition that it was part of an old Roman road from Stockport to Warrington, but hard evidence of such antiquity has yet to be found. The natural assumption from the name 'Glebelands' is that much of the land on either side belonged to the rector of St. Martin's as 'glebe lands'. In fact this is not the case. The rector owned one small strip of land on the south side of Glebelands Road. Except for two other fields, all the land on either side of Glebelands Road belonged to Bowdon parish. St. Martin's glebe lands were much nearer to Ashton village, on either side of Dumber Lane, so the name 'Glebelands Road' possibly meant "the road leading from the village through the glebe lands". This supports the view that at the time Dumber Lane was regarded as part of Glebelands Road. By 1876 it had become 'Park Lane' and the name 'Dumber Lane' first appears in the street directory for 1893. Older inhabitants of Ashton still refer to "going down the Dumber". There were no houses or buildings in Dumber Lane in 1841, but a white obelisk stood in the corner of the glebe field opposite the modern Wellfield Junior School. The rector of St. Martin's from 1774 to 1835, the Rev. Popplewell Johnson, was a keen huntsman and erected the obelisk in memory of his horse, Una, and his pointer dog, Norma. The obelisk was destroyed in 1934 when houses were built on the site.

Glebelands Road was merely a cart track. Near the Cross Street end was 'Chapel Field', where the first non-conformist chapel in the two townships was built (see the section on 'Cross Street'). There were only four houses along Glebelands Road, two on the south side and two on the north side. It is not possible to name the occupants of two of the houses in 1841 as the names of the occupiers in the Tithe Apportionment do not appear in the census. Three of the houses were owned by Isaac Barrett, who lived on Cross Street. Two of them were situated where Glen Avenue joins Glebelands Road today. They were rented by Thomas Albinson and Samuel Goody in 1845. Opposite was the home of Peter Irlam. He was a coal labourer, aged 44 and lived with his wife, Mary, and their grown-up daughter.

There was a path leading from Glebelands Road to Ashton Lane, roughly along the line of the present Park Road. Halfway along this path, in the middle of the fields, were two houses on the site of the modern Park Road School playing field. One of them was named 'Park House', which took its name from the large 15-acre field ('Park Field') lying between it and the main road. The house was the home of Thomas Higginson, a man aged 53 'of independent means'. Both he and his wife Ellen came from outside Cheshire. Nearby was the farmhouse of Amos Ogden. He was 75 and lived with his younger brother Robert. Amos owned the farm, which consisted of two fields next to the farmhouse and three on the north side of Glebelands Road.

The last house in Glebelands Road was 'Woodfield Cottage', opposite the modern Ashton Park. This was the home of James Alcock, a 71-year old 'farmer'. He died in July 1842, and in the Tithe Apportionment his widow Martha still rented the house and garden, but no farm fields.

10. Marsland Road

Marsland Road derives its name from the Marsland family who had two farms on the east side of the canal near Brooklands Bridge. It seems probable that the bridge over the canal (formerly called 'Marsland's Bridge', now 'Brooklands Bridge') was built after the canal was originally constructed. It is not shown on two maps of 1770-1777, but is shown on a map of the canal dated 1785-90. The George Legh Estate map of 1801 shows that Marsland Road originally joined Washway Road further north, in the region of Urban Road. In 1841 the section from Sale Moor to approximately the end of Derbyshire Road was called 'New Lane', indicating its more recent origin. The rest of the road was probably called 'Marsland's Lane', although the 1867 Rate Book also refers to a road at the Brooklands end as 'Boggart Lane'. In 1867 the name 'Marsland Road' was applied to the whole of the road from Washway Road to Sale Moor; 'New Lane', however, continued to be listed in the rate books for another four years. Although the final 's' of 'Marsland's' has officially been dropped over a hundred and twenty years ago, it is still heard today from older people.

Between Washway Road and the canal bridge there were fields on each side of the road; some of these were cultivated, others had cattle grazing in them (the cemetery was not created until 1862). The land on both sides belonged to a number of owners, each of whom had received several parcels of land when the Moor was enclosed in 1807. The bridge itself was very narrow, just wide enough for a horse and cart to pass over it in comfort.

There were only four houses on the north side of Marsland Road between Marsland's Bridge and the junction with Northenden Road a mile away. The first was on the corner of Wardle Road and Marsland Road. This was a farm belonging to Robert Marsland. The farm was the home of his mother, Anne, who was 67 and had one servant living with her. The farm lands were five fields at the back of the house. It seems probable that Robert's father, Edward Marsland, had left the farm to his son in his will, with the proviso that his widow Anne should be allowed to live there for the rest of her life. Near the junction with Derbyshire Road were two cottages, one in the course of being built. The completed one was the home of James Bardsley, an agricultural worker in his fifties. In addition to his wife Alice, three sons and three other labourers lived with him. James rented two or three fields behind the cottage. The last building on the north side of the road was situated around the junction of the modern Alexandra Road. It was the home of sixteen people, including William Bardsley, a farmer in his thirties, his wife and two small children.

We shall now return to Brooklands Bridge and look at the south side of Marsland Road. The scene to the south of the road was completely rural; Brooklands Road was not built until about 1859. About two hundred yards to the south of the bridge were several buildings approached by a track leading from the bridge. To the east of the track was the cottage of John Kelsall, a 53-year old agricultural worker. His wife, Sarah, and their two children lived with him, plus one female servant. John rented two fields near his house, but probably worked on 'Bridge Farm' next door. The track itself led to this farm, which was rented by Robert Marsland from Lawrence Wright. The Marslands had farmed in this area for over 70 years. 43-years old Robert was away from home on the day of the census, but his first wife, Sarah, two children, five servants and two agricultural workers were at home. Sarah died in 1843 and Robert married again. The farm was one of the largest in Sale – 154 acres, plus 54 acres in the neighbouring parish of Baguley. When the area was named 'Brooklands', about 1860, the farm became 'Brooklands Farm'. Robert retired and the farm was leased to Roger Hillkirk from Tideswell in Derbyshire; for many years it was known locally as 'Hillkirk's Farm'. The farm buildings were situated between the modern Acre Field and Kirklands (off Framingham Road), while the farm lands covered the area between the modern Walton Road (on the west), Alcester Road (on the east), Marsland Road (on the north) and Baguley Brook (on the south). The line of the western boundary leads to the conclusion that the farm was in existence before the Bridgewater Canal was built. Button Brook ran within a few yards of the farm buildings on its way from Northenden to the River Mersey. Although Robert Marsland rented his large farm, he actually owned the smaller farm at the corner of Wardle Road and Marsland Road, as already mentioned; in addition to this he owned a house on Northenden Road.

There were only two sets of buildings between Brooklands Road and Derbyshire Road South. A triangle of land opposite the site of the modern Independent Insurance building belonged to Sale Township. The area was called 'Langley', and consisted of three fields and two

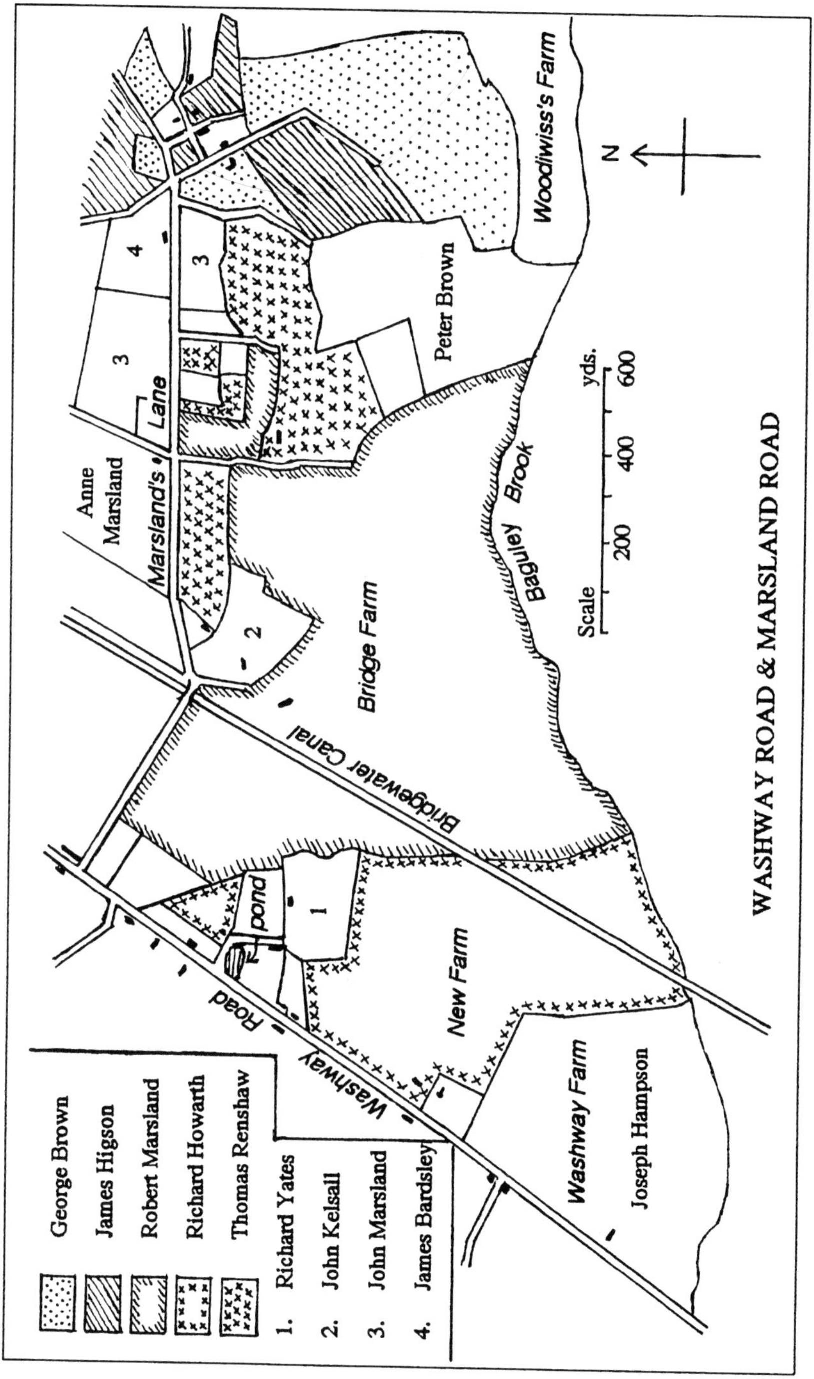
George Brown
James Higson
Robert Marsland
Richard Howarth
Thomas Renshaw
1. Richard Yates
2. John Kelsall
3. John Marsland
4. James Bardsley
Woodiwiss's Farm
N
Peter Brown
Anne Marsland
Marsland's Lane
Bridge Farm
Baguley Brook
Scale
200
400
600
yds.
Bridgewater Canal
pond
New Farm
Washway Road
Washway Farm
Joseph Hampson

WASHWAY ROAD & MARSLAND ROAD

cottages – the poor house. Here lived eleven people, including two widows and their families. The cottages were in a very bad condition and in June 1842 the Vestry meeting decided to 'put them into good repair'. Opposite the end of Wardle Road, a track led down to the buildings of Williamson's Farm (this track later became George's Road). The farm (later called 'Whitehall Farm') had been established for over a hundred years and was rented in 1841 by Thomas Renshaw from Rev. John Hunter, the curate of St. Martin's in Ashton-upon-Mersey. The latter in turn had it on lease from Samuel Brooks, who had purchased the farm and lands for £3150 in 1829. Thomas was 53 and in 1841 was one of the Surveyors of the Highways. He lived with his wife, Elizabeth, and their seven children. The farm lands covered a large area to the south of Marsland Road, and included fields which later formed the southern half of the 'Moorfield Botanical Gardens'.

Derbyshire Road South was a short path leading into the fields. Near the junction with Marsland Road was an area known as 'Moor Nook', a name which still survives in a short cul-de-sac. In 1841 Moor Nook consisted of two farms and several houses. The first farm was that of George Brown, who was in his sixties. His wife, Margaret, his son William and his family, and two agricultural labourers lived with him. The farm, which included an orchard next to the house, was leased from Thomas Baxter, and stretched from Marsland Road right down to Baguley Brook. The second farm was on the east side of the lane and was leased from the Legh Estate by James Higson. In addition to the farm and fourteen fields, James also rented two other houses and two fields, which he sub-let to others. He was also co-owner with his brother Jacob of a row of houses in Sale Green, which they let out. James was in his forties, and lived with his six children and two servants. His brother Jacob, who was a market gardener, lived in one of the other houses at Moor Nook. His house was leased by James and sub-let to him. Jacob was 38 and had a wife and three children. The other inhabitants of Moor Nook totalled 52 in number, and included another market gardener (by the name of John Kelsall), a tailor, a blacksmith, a weaver, a hot-plater, and several agricultural labourers. The last building on the south side of Marsland Road was a large house almost facing the junction with Northenden Road. At the time of the Tithe Apportionment it was occupied by another John Kelsall (a farmer), but in the census he was living in Northenden Road in the house of Martha Barlow. The inhabitants in 1841 were four agricultural labourers with their families.

11. School Road and Chapel Road

School Road

School Road is now regarded as the centre of Sale; the shops, the Metrolink station and the shopping precinct are the hub around which the whole town revolves. In 1841 this was far from the case. A person standing in Washway Road looking up School Lane (as it was called until 1867) would see a narrow entrance (about half as wide as it is now); on the right they would see only four buildings along the whole of the 400 yards up to the canal, and on the left five. The rest consisted of fields of oats, wheat, and vegetables. Some idea of the rural nature of the area may be gained from the fact that in 1830 the Township Vestry commented on the nuisance caused by people who unloaded manure in School Lane and Chapel Lane and left it there. In future it would be moved "within three days"!

The first house on the right-hand side, a long, narrow building, was the home of William Davenport, a wheelwright, who lived with his wife Elizabeth and a teenage servant. The next house was the home of John Heywood, a farmer in his seventies. He lived with his wife, Martha, an unmarried daughter, and a female servant. John also owned two cottages at the canal end of Roebuck Lane. There was a gap of 230 yards on the right hand side between John Heywood's house and the next building, the school. This gap was taken up by three fields and a large pond, which was situated in front of a clump of trees between the modern Hereford Street and Boots the Chemists. Halfway between the Mall and Springfield Road was the township school, a stone building built around 1806-7. Here the children of Sale were educated, the total number of pupils being around 50 at any one time. The schoolmaster in 1841 was 36-year old James Warren; he lived on the school premises, with his wife Anne and their four small children. James, born in Baguley, had been appointed schoolmaster in Sale in May 1836. He rented two fields near the school. Between the school and the canal was a small cottage set back from the road. This also belonged to Sale Township and was the home of Elizabeth Lightfoot (a 70-year old widow), William Shaw (an agricultural labourer) with his wife and 3 children, and a 20-year old lodger, Ellen Royle.

At the top of School Road was Sale Bridge, which until the coming of the railway was hump-backed and very narrow, about a fifth of the width of the modern bridge. It was probably just wide enough for two horses and carts to pass on it. Beyond the bridge, the road to Northenden ran through what used to be 'the Moor' (see p.4).

If we were now to return down the north side of School Road back towards Washway Road, the first building to be seen was on the site of the present Civic Theatre. This was the Independent (Congregational) Chapel, which had been built in 1805. In 1841 the fortunes of the chapel were at a very low ebb. Its minister, the Rev. Samuel Gibbon, left during the year and the chapel was closed for a short time in 1842. The coming of a new minister revitalised the congregation, and they were able to move to new premises in Montague Road in 1852. Adjoining the chapel was a small house where William Alderley lived with his wife Sarah. William, the brother of Samuel Alderley of Wallbank Farm, was 65, and a man of independent means (in addition to owning the house in School Road he rented a house near Sale Green, which he then let to his son William). The next house was that of John Chapman, a 51-year old coal dealer. He made a living by unloading coal when it arrived by barge on the canal, and then distributing it to houses and farms in the area. Originally from Eccles, he lived with his wife Lois and their five children. The next 280 yards (almost three-quarters of the total length of School Road) was taken up by fields and gardens, with the exception of two houses halfway down, nearly opposite the pond. These both belonged to Mary Leeds. In one of them lived Anne Leeds, a 64-year old lady of independent means, with two grown-up children and a female servant. In the other lived Mary Clarke. She was in her forties and came from Scotland; she had four servants living in.

Approaching the main road once more, we would first come to the house rented by Thomas Cookson, a market gardener. He was 58 years old, and lived with his teenage daughter. In the same house lived Isaac Bithell, labourer, with his wife Hannah and their 5 children, and Sarah Dickinson, another market gardener of the same age as Thomas. Their gardens were round the house itself, although Thomas also owned three other houses, an orchard and three fields right at the far end of Sale. These were all rented out to others. At the corner, opposite the Davenports' house, was the 'Bull's Head', occupying the same location as it does today (see the section on 'Cross Street').

Because of the rural nature of the area, a person standing halfway up School Road would have been able to see at least as far as Raglan Road to the south, and right up to Dane Road to the north. The only houses between these were two in Chapel Road (to the north) and two in Roebuck Lane (to the south).

Chapel Road

The entrance to Chapel Road was much wider than the entrances to both School Road and Dane Road. Chapel Road ('Chapel Lane' in 1841) took its name from the Unitarian chapel which stood between Leicester Road and Joynson Street. This chapel ('Cross Street Chapel') was originally built by the Presbyterians in 1739 and superseded the one in Glebelands Road. The land belonged to Thomas Atkinson and also contained 'Ashfield House' (see the section on 'Cross Street'). By 1777 the congregation had changed their beliefs and a Unitarian minister was appointed. It became a Sunday school in 1876, when a new Unitarian chapel was opened in Atkinson Road. The building was demolished in 1972 and three town-houses were built on the site.

There were two houses on the north side of Chapel Road. The first, near the junction with Cross Street, was rented by Sarah Massey. She was a school-teacher around fifty years of age. Probably she taught at Jane Bellott's School for Ladies just along Cross Street. She had two sons (agricultural labourers) living with her. The second house was further up Chapel Road, about where Symons Road joins it today. This was the home of Abraham Hewitt, a farmer in his thirties. He lived with four children and a female servant. The farm consisted of four fields next to the house and six other fields scattered to the south. Abraham also owned a row of cottages situated near the canal, opposite the modern 'Railway Inn'. These were called 'Cabbage Row', later 'Sale Cottages'. Thirty-three people lived in the cottages, including two boatmen, two warehousemen, a shoemaker, a bricklayer and four agricultural labourers, all with their families. The bricklayer and shoemaker even had servants.

It is difficult to imagine it today, but there were no buildings on the south side of Chapel Road between the chapel (near Cross street) and the canal. The area consisted of fields and gardens. Near the canal Chapel Road turned south to meet School Road, as it does today. People used to collect along this part of the road to see the busy traffic on the canal, or to watch boats being unloaded on the other side (at the time, there was no wall to block their view). Facing the canal there were two houses. One was at right angles to the canal; this was the home of Abel Chapman, a boatman in his twenties. He lived with his wife and child. Another family with six children also lived with them. The second house faced the canal. Here lived Peter Heywood (or Heward), a coal dealer. He was 47 and had a wife and five children.

12. Northenden Road

The present-day Northenden Road stretches 1¾ miles from Sale Bridge to the boundary with Northenden. Until 1867 it was considered to be two distinct roads, 'Moor Lane' (from Sale Bridge to Wythenshawe Road) and 'Hart Lane'.

From Sale Bridge to Sale Moor

This was called 'Moor Lane', because it ran along the northern edge of 'The Moor' (see p.4). Very few buildings were at first built in this area but the coming of the railway in 1849 changed this, as the businessmen who commuted to Manchester preferred to build their villas and houses near the railway station.

Near the bridge, on the site of the present 'Queen's Hotel', was the house of James Royle, a carrier now 67 years old. Nineteen other people lived in the house, mostly relations. Alongside the canal was a track leading through to Marsland Road. This later became 'Hope Road', being named after James Hope, a previous owner of the land. The track had to be re-routed slightly to the east in 1849 in accommodate the railway, which now ran between it and the canal. On the opposite side of Northenden Road, Broad Road ran away to the northeast on its present alignment, but the triangle of land enclosed by Northenden Road, Broad Road and Woodlands Road was thick with trees – this was 'White's Wood' (it belonged to Captain John White). It was the home of many birds, rabbits and other small animals, as was a second wood on Irlam Road.

Walking down Northenden Road towards the junction with Marsland Road, we would be able to see over the fields to Dane Road on the left and to Marsland Road on the right. In between the bridge and the 'Temple', at the corner of Temple Road, there were two buildings, one on each side of the road. The rest consisted of fields and hedges. Wardle Road (constructed after the 1807 enclosures) led through to Marsland Road. At the time it was called 'Moss's Lane'. Looking along it we would see one building – the farm of Peter Wardle. The house became known as 'Wardle House' and later gave its name to the road – 'Wardle Lane'; this in turn became 'Wardle Road' in 1867. Although the house has been demolished, its name may still be read on the stone gateposts near the end of Broomville Avenue. Peter Wardle was 53

Sale Green Cottages, Sale.

Sale Green Cottages. For hundreds of years the 'centre' of Sale was Sale Green. These cottages stood from circa 1690 to 1937. (Photograph reproduced here by courtesy of Trafford Local Studies Centre.)

and lived with his wife, Mary, and two labourers, who helped him on his 11-acre farm.

Between Wardle Road and Derbyshire Road stood a small cottage belonging to Edward Marsland. He was in his thirties, with a wife and three small children. In the census he described himself as a 'farmer', but, according to the Tithe Apportionment, he had only one large field, next to the house. A farm labourer also lived in the cottage, with his wife and baby boy. The cottage is still lived in today, although enlarged into three cottages. After the Crimean War, the cottages took the name 'Inkerman Cottages', and later were the home of Luke Winstanley, the Sale builder.

Derbyshire Road also led through to Marsland Road. Looking down it we would see the house of John Darbyshire, a hay-dealer and agricultural labourer in his sixties, who presumably gave his name to the road. In addition to John's wife Elizabeth, another labourer, a widow and a brickmaker all lived there with their respective families. The house, which is still there today, later became a smithy. There were two other houses on the south side of Northenden road, between the modern Warrener Street and the end of Marsland Road. In these lived James Greaves (coal dealer), George Leeds (smallware maufacturer) and Thomas Gurden (commission agent) with their respective families and servants.

On the north side of Moor Lane (Northenden Road) the farm of James Woodall was situated just before the modern Clarendon Road. He was 58 and his household consisted of wife, Betty, and their three children. He farmed 10 acres and employed one labourer. The farm was rented from William Woodall, possibly James's brother. In 1841 'Temple Lane' stretched only as far as Broad Road; the remaining section was 'Finch Lane'. The 'Temple', the large building at the corner of Northenden Road, had been there for some years; the origin of its name has not yet been discovered. In 1841 the building housed four families. Three of these were agricultural labourers; the fourth was a blacksmith, Thomas Skellan. By the time of the Tithe Apportionment, Thomas Skellan had moved to the corner of Marsland Road, premises which were later extended and became well-known as John Wood's general store. Between Temple Road and the end of Marsland Road was a large house belonging to Martha Barlow. She was 58, of independent means, and had two nephews and a servant living with her. Also in the house was John Kelsall, a 60-year-old farmer with his wife and three children.

Sale Moor to Wythenshawe Road

As already mentioned, this was part of 'Moor Lane' until 1867. On the north side of the road between the Old Hall Road junction and Baguley Road, there were two buildings called the 'Barracks'. As explained in the section dealing with Carrington Lane, in 1841 this word was not limited to military use, but could describe any temporary buildings. The inhabitants of the 'Barracks' seem to have been mostly elderly people, including 68-year-old John Tyrer (butcher, father of the innkeeper of the 'Bull's Head'), his wife, a son and two servants, John Critchlow (a weaver) and Phoebe Aldcroft, a lady of independent means. There were two houses in the next section between Baguley Road and Wythenshawe Road. These belonged to William Dewsbury of Lime Tree Farm and were rented out. The occupier of the first house, a farm later known as 'Victoria Farm', was William Walkden. He was aged 45 and lived with his wife and their six children. Two agricultural workers with their families also lived in. The farm was later rented by Thomas Marsland, who in 1841 lived opposite the end of Wythenshawe Road. The other house was the home of John Alderley (shopkeeper) and two agricultural labourers, all with their families. Further along there were two large ponds and the Primitive Methodist Chapel built in 1839. This was replaced in 1873 by a larger building on the same site.

The first two buildings on the south side of the road after the junction with Marsland Road were two cottages. The first was the home of Thomas Brickell, a wheelwright. Aged 39, he lived with his wife, Mary, two teenage children and a teenage servant. The second cottage was leased by Sarah Goodier, a widow with four children. By 1846 Thomas Brickell was also a 'beer-seller' and in the 1851 census he was a 'wheelwright and inn-keeper'. This was the 'Legh Arms'; the name refers of course to the Legh family of East Legh Hall, High Legh, who owned much of the land in this part of Sale, including the plot on which the 'Legh Arms' was situated. Opposite the 'Barracks' was the house of John Cordingley, a farmer and one of the Assessors of Assessed Taxes in 1841. He rented eight fields near the house and another near Wardle Road. He had a wife and eight children (from 15 years down to 3 months).

Today Baguley Road is split into two parts; the shorter northern section is a very busy road linking Old Hall Road and Northenden Road. The southern section remains a track and retains its old name of 'Baguley Lane'. In the nineteenth century a favourite Sunday pastime was walking the three-quarters of a mile down to Baguley Brook, at the southern end of the lane. On the way, the walkers passed two farms. The first was Shawcross's Farm (later 'Lime Tree Farm'), rented by William Dewsbury. Aged around 50, he had ten children living with him, and one agricultural labourer. The thirteen fields of the farm were all on the east side of Baguley Lane. The second farm, Woodiwiss's Farm (later 'Beech Farm'), was down a short track which diverged not far from the township boundary. This farm was rented by John Hampson, aged 55. He had thirteen fields on the west side of Baguley Lane, and lived with his wife, Sarah, and seven children.

Between Baguley Lane and Gratrix Lane there were four houses. In the first two lived Elizabeth Whitehead (a lady of independent means), John Eckersley (a weaver), John Holland (farmer) and Mary Renshaw (a widow). John Holland rented three fields at the back of his house. Roughly on the site of the present Blakemere Avenue was another farm, approached by a track along the line of the modern Sunningdale Avenue. This belonged to James Renshaw; the occupant in 1841 is not clear from the census. It was rented out to a William Renshaw in the Tithe Apportionment. Lastly came the farm of Thomas Marsland. The farmhouse and garden were situated opposite the end of the modern Heathfield Close; the five fields were on the other side of the road. Thomas was in 42 years old and lived with his wife, Ann, and a female servant.

Gratrix Lane took its name from the Gr(e)atrix family who owned land in the area. The lane was a cul-de-sac, following the line of the modern Gratrix Lane and Sandbach Road. Near the junction of these two roads were the farm buildings of Peter Greatrix. He was 71 years old, and owned seven fields near his house. Peter was retired and the farm was now run by his son, John (aged 33), who lived with him. Their two wives, one other son and two labourers completed the household. Right at the southern end of the lane was Holly Hey Farm (written as 'Ollen High' in the census). This was owned by James Woodall. who was aged 37, living with his wife, Charlotte, and two young children.

Wythenshawe Road to the Northenden boundary

This part of the road was called 'Hart Lane' until 1867, when the name was changed to 'Northenden Road'. The old name, however, persisted for seven years in the Rate Books.

At the corner of Wythenshawe Road and Northenden Road was a shop and garden rented by John Sutherland. He lived with his wife, Mary, and six children. They had one teenage servant. The house is still inhabited today. Not far from it was the 'Carter's Arms'. The occupier in 1841 is not clear, but by the time of the Tithe Apportionment, it was Obadiah Leigh (see below). After the 'Carter's Arms' there were two houses. The first was owned by John Bennett, a 65-year old weaver who lived with his son, Timothy, and the latter's family. The second house was owned by John Renshaw, another weaver, aged 50. In his house lived his wife, Hannah, three children, another weaver with his wife and seven children, and two agricultural labourers with their families. Opposite John Sutherland's shop was the house of Edward Greatrix and his wife Elizabeth. Edward was 38 years old and was described as a farmer, but, as he rented only one field, the 1851 census description ('a market gardener') was probably more accurate. His 62-year old father, also called Edward, lived with him. In the 1851 census, the latter was described as a 'beer-house keeper' (the house was later the 'Lindow Tavern'). A widow, Martha Marsland, also lived there. The total household comprised twelve people, including three small children. A few yards further along the road was a large house which housed 33 people. One of these was William Hall, a tailor, the son of the William Hall living in Buck Lane, Ashton-upon-Mersey. The younger William was 40 and had a wife and five children. Another was Obadiah Leigh, a weaver, who later became a beer-seller in premises on the other side of the road (see above). His wife, Dinah, looked after several nurse-children. The next house was the home of Mary Cookson. She was 68, of independent means, living with her twenty-five-year old daughter. Close to the boundary with Northenden was the aptly-named 'Boundary House', the home of Paul Marple, a 'proprietor of houses'. Born in Staveley (Derbyshire) he was a widower, 64 years old, living with his 34-year old daughter. In 1841 he was one of the elected Overseers of the Poor.

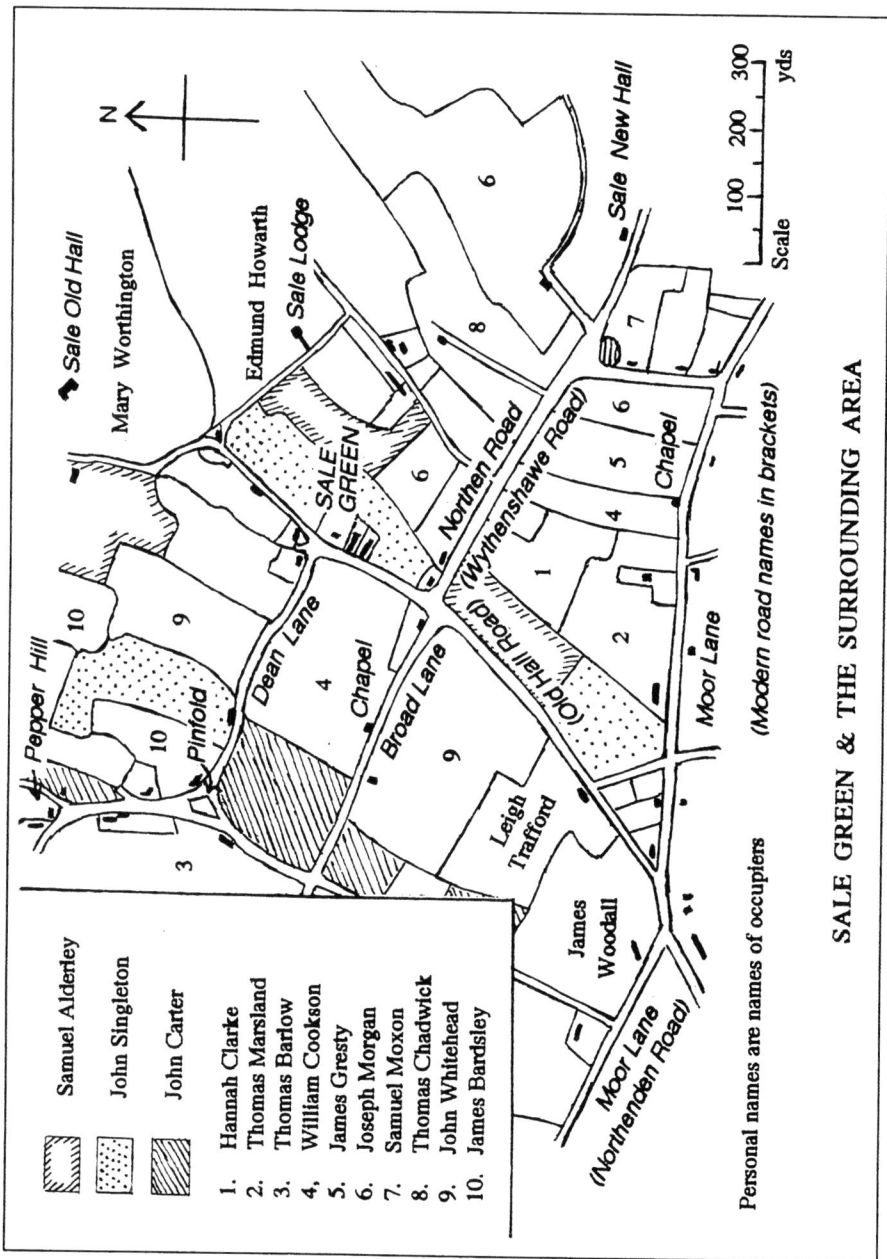

SALE GREEN & THE SURROUNDING AREA

Sale Old Hall

Mary Worthington

Edmund Howarth

Sale Lodge

SALE GREEN

Northen Road

(Wythenshawe Road)

(Old Hall Road)

Chapel

Pepper Hill

Pinfold

Dean Lane

Chapel

Broad Lane

Leigh Trafford

Moor Lane

Sale New Hall

James Woodall

Moor Lane (Northenden Road)

Scale

100   200   300
yds

Personal names are names of occupiers

(Modern road names in brackets)

Samuel Alderley

John Singleton

John Carter

1. Hannah Clarke
2. Thomas Marsland
3. Thomas Barlow
4. William Cookson
5. James Gresty
6. Joseph Morgan
7. Samuel Moxon
8. Thomas Chadwick
9. John Whitehead
10. James Bardsley

13. Broad Road and Old Hall Road

Broad Road

Until 1867 Broad Road was 'Broad Lane'. As Norman Swain pointed out, it is probable that it originally joined Washway Road via the modern Dargle Road, near the end of Dane Road. Diverting Broad Road to Sale Bridge removed the need to build another bridge over the canal.

There were two houses on the east side of the canal, north of Sale Bridge. As the towpath was on the west side, the approach to the houses was through the fields at the side of Broad Road. One of the houses was called 'New House' in the census. This was the home of William Chapman, a gardener. His wife, Olive, and grown-up son lived with him. William had a field near his house and also looked after the garden of the Independent Chapel on the other side of the canal. The other house was partly a warehouse, and here lived Elizabeth Atkinson, an oil merchant, with one servant. It seems likely that Elizabeth was married; if this was the case, her husband was away at the time of the census.

Along the whole length of Broad Road, from Northenden Road to Old Hall Road, there were only four buildings, plus one farm set back from the road. The farm was 'Clark's Hey', named after one of the fields belonging to the farm. The farm buildings were situated at the end of a private road, which ran along the line of the modern Lynwood Grove, opposite Irlam Road. The farm lands consisted of six fields between Broad Road and the canal, plus one other field in the area between Dane Road and the Mersey. The farm was rented by William Smith, a man aged 45, who lived with his wife and six children.

The cottage of William Kelsall was situated on the south side of Broad Road, between Clarendon Road and Temple Road. William was an agricultural labourer in his thirties. His wife and two children made up the household. Between Temple Road and Old Hall Lane was the farm of John Whitehead (later known as 'Yewtree Cottage'). The farm and its lands were rented from George C. Legh. In addition to the seventeen fields he rented, John owned a house and two fields near Baguley Road, where his mother lived. John was aged 44 and was one of the Overseers of the Poor. His household consisted of himself, his wife, their two children, and four servants. Opposite the farm buildings was a large pond, and next to the pond was Broad Road Wesleyan Chapel, the first Methodist chapel in Sale. It was opened in August 1820; forty years later it was clear that the 'centre' of Sale had moved to School Road, and many members left to found a new church there. Worship continued at Broad Road until the chapel was finally closed in 1875. The last building was near the junction with Old Hall Road. It was a smithy and garden, which Thomas Barlow (of Temple Farm) leased from John Moore. As the smithy seems to have been purely a place of work rather than a dwelling-place, the name of the smith in 1841 is not known, but it was possibly John Aldcroft, who lived on Northenden Road.

Old Hall Road

Old Hall Road was, of course, the road leading from Northenden Road to the Old Hall. It is possible that it had no name before 'Old Hall Road' was introduced in 1867, although there is some evidence that the section from Dane Road towards the Old Hall was called 'Massey Lane'.

In 1841 there was one large house in the section between Northenden Road and the crossroads at the end of Broad Road. This was Sale Cottage, which stood opposite the end of Baguley Road. It was owned by Henry Leigh Trafford, a magistrate with chambers in St. James's Square, Manchester. He also owned two fields near the house, and rented a large field behind the house from George C. Legh. He was in his forties and lived with his wife, Eliza, and their five children. They had six servants to run the house for them. In 1851 we find the family living at 'Belmont' on Bury New Road, Salford.

The area around the junctions of Dane Road with Old Hall Road and Broad Road was known as 'Sale Green'. This was the centre of Sale for hundreds of years until the building of the railway caused the centre to move to School Road and the railway station. There were two rows of cottages at right angles to the road, and these ('Sale Green Cottages') were home to 64 people. Most of them were agricultural labourers or weavers, with their families. The cottages were built towards the end of the eighteenth century, and were finally demolished in 1937-8. Next to the cottages was the house and garden of William Perrin, a market gardener, aged 48. He had a wife and two children to support. Further up, on the other (west) side of the road, there were two houses. The first was the home of James Clarke and his wife Hannah. He was a farmer and rented three fields on the south side of Wythenshawe Road. He was 81 years of age and died three months after the census was taken. The second house was rented by Jonathan Brownhill. He was an agricultural labourer aged 52, living with his wife and six children. He supplemented his income by being the official 'mole-catcher' (see p.6).

The last set of buildings on the west side of the road were those of Wallbank Farm. It was one of the largest farms in Sale, and was rented by Samuel Alderley from John White. Samuel was 53 and lived with his wife, Sarah, their four children and three servants. In 1841 Samuel was one of the Surveyors of the Highways. The farm lands were extensive, covering twenty-five rented fields plus four other fields owned by Samuel himself. The fields were mostly near the farm buildings, but some were between Broad Road and Northenden Road (presumably allocated when the Moor was enclosed in 1807) and others were by the River Mersey.

On the opposite side of the road, between Wallbank Farm and Jonathan Brownhill's house, was 'Howarth's Lodge'. Here lived John Renshaw (aged 56) and his wife, Ann. The lodge was at the entrance to a large house called 'Sale Lodge'. The latter was a large mansion, described in White's *1860 Gazetteer of Cheshire* as 'a handsome stone residence'. It was built around 1830 for Edmund Howarth, a retired merchant. Born in Blackburn, he had come to live in Sale and had brought four servants with him. He was a widower, and in 1841 was aged 76. In the 1851 census we find his son Edmund, a magistrate, living there as well. Edmund the father owned the small lodge where the Renshaws lived, the house where Jonathan Browhill lived, a number of houses in the area (called 'Howarth's houses') and thirteen fields, some of which he rented out to tenants. In 1854 he was instrumental in starting a school for children of the neighbourhood. Sale Lodge still survives as part of the club-house of Sale Golf Club.

The last building on the east side of the road was Sale Old Hall, which was approached by means of a drive starting near John Renshaw's lodge. The hall was E-shaped, and faced south-west. It was situated near the north side of the roundabout at Junction 8 of the M63 motorway. It was the original seat of the Massey family (the lords of the manor), and the building of 1600 probably replaced an earlier manor-house. In 1840 the hall was bought by Mrs. Mary Worthington. She was the daughter of the Rev. Robert Harrop of Hale Barns and

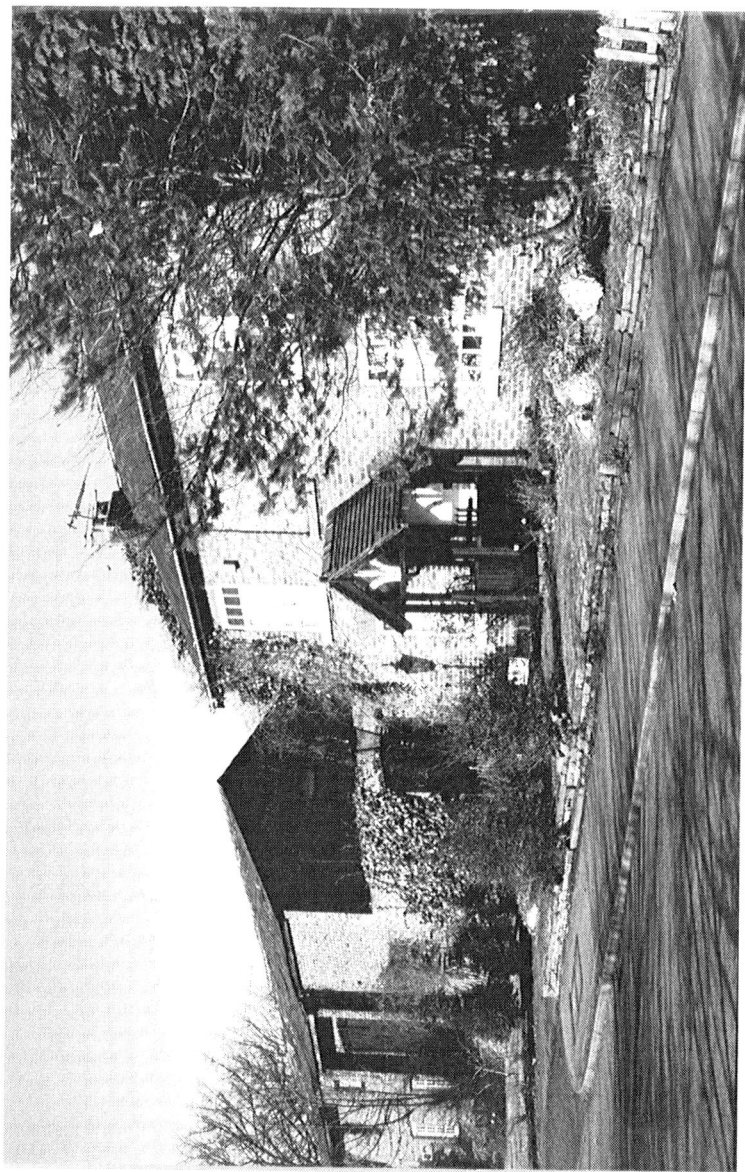

Temple Farm (see p.80). (Photograph by the author.)

lived in Altrincham with her husband, Hugo, attorney and legal adviser to the Earl of Stamford at Dunham Hall. When her husband died in November, 1839, she decided to move to Sale, possibly because her son Robert was a solicitor with a share in a practice in Manchester. The hall was being used as a school and was in a poor state of repair. Mrs. Worthington had it repaired and rebuilt. In the 1841 census we find her in residence with three grown-up children. In addition to eight servants and a gardener, there were three other friends or relatives staying there at the time. Mrs. Worthington appears to have died in 1844-5 and in the Tithe Apportionment we find her elder son Robert as owner. By 1848 he had moved to Crumpsall Hall and the hall in Sale was let to several wealthy tenants until the younger son James returned from China in 1864 and took up residence. The hall was eventually demolished in 1920.

14. Wythenshawe Road and Fairy Lane

Wythenshawe Road

Although no name is given in the 1841 census, we know from contemporary directories that Wythenshawe Road was called 'Northen Lane' or 'Road' until the new name was introduced in 1867. 'Northen' was the old name for Northenden, so the name 'Northen Road' confirms that the original route to Northenden before Sale Moor was enclosed lay via Dane Road and Wythenshawe Road. Fairy Lane ran off to the east at the bend in Wythenshawe Road. The name of the western section of Fairy Lane was changed to 'New Hall Road' in 1867.

There were two houses on Wythenshawe Road near the junction with Old Hall Road. It is not possible to discover the names of the occupants in 1841; in the Tithe Apportionment, one of the houses was a farm occupied by Edward Gresty, but at the time of the census he was a weaver, living on Northenden Road. Down Rutland Lane ('Davenport Lane' in 1841) there were three sets of houses, two on the west side and one on the east. All three sets of houses belonged to Edmund Howarth of Sale Lodge. The first on the left ('Marsland's houses') were the homes of Thomas Brownhill and James Carter. They were both labourers and probably worked on Edmund Howarth's land. Thomas had a wife and ten children, while James had wife and three children. The second set of houses was rented by Elizabeth Marsland, a lady of independent means in her seventies. She lived with her son. Another family with four children also lived with them. Facing the Marslands were three houses. They housed James Cookson, a gardener (aged 44), Thomas Cookson, a coachman (aged 45), and John Alderley, an agricultural labourer (aged 40), with their families. Near the bend where Fairy Lane diverged, a lane ran off to the left. This led to Astle's Farm (later 'The Oaks'). The tenant in 1841 was Thomas Chadwick, a farmer aged around 50, living with his wife, two children and a servant. Three other families appear to have lived in. The farm lands consisted of four fields round the house. At the corner of Wythenshawe Road and Fairy Lane was a large pond. Near it, in Wythenshawe Road, were two more houses, the homes of James Jackson and Samuel Moxon. James was an agricultural worker, aged about 30. He had a wife and four children.

Samuel Moxon was a man of independent means, in his fifties. He lived with his wife, Mary, and two servants.

Fairy Lane

Fairy Lane was cut in two by the M63 motorway in 1974 and had to be re-aligned.

Not far down Fairy Lane, a track led off to the left to Gratrix's Farm (so called because the owner was George Gratrix). On later maps the farm is called 'Shevington House'. The tenant in 1841 was Joseph Morgan, a farmer aged 41. His wife, Frances, four children and one servant made up the household. Joseph employed 5 men to help him with the farm. Sale New Hall was the next building. This was built in 1688 by William Massey and the farm attached to it was one of the largest in Sale, covering over 124 acres. The farm was rented from John White by Sarah Whitelegg, aged 77. She had three relations and six servants living with her. She died in January, 1844, and the farm was then let to Thomas Barlow, whom we have already met at Temple Farm. Sale New Hall was demolished in May, 1953. Fairy Lane petered out in the fields at the east end of the township, and a path led to two farms near the Northenden boundary. One was Lyth's Farm (later 'Oak House' or 'Fairy Lane Farm'). This was rented by John Strettell, who lived with his wife and one teenage servant. The other farm was Waterside Farm, which was rented by Peter Greatrix, the son of the Peter Greatrix of Gratrix Lane. He was 36, and had a wife and five children. They had a teenage servant to help in the house. The eight farm fields were situated round the house. There is one more house listed in the census – 'Waterside House'. This was probably a house next to the Farm. It was the home of a weaver and two agricultural labourers, with their families. The house was part of the Sale New Hall estate, and we may assume the labourers worked on that farm.

Dane Road Farm (see p.79). (Photograph by the author.)

15. Dane Road

Dane Road was originally 'Dean Lane' ('the road running along the valley', the valley being that of the River Mersey). The road did not lie in the valley itself, because the river often overflowed and flooded the valley floor. Instead the road ran along the edge of the valley, roughly three-eighths of a mile south of the river. Dane Road was part of the route from Stockport to Warrington, and tradition says that it was originally Roman, although no concrete evidence has yet been discovered. In 1867 'Dean Lane' was changed to the present 'Dane Road', although 'Dean Road' persisted in the Rate Books until the 1880's.

At the narrow entrance to Dane Road from Cross Street lay Manor Farm. This is dealt with in the section relating to Cross Street. The bridge over the canal was known as 'White's Bridge', taking its name from Dr. Thomas White, the surgeon who lived at Sale Priory when the canal was built. On either side of the bridge there was a building. The one on the west side was a smithy, the home of James Brownhill. His household consisted of his wife, Sarah, their three young children and one female servant. Sarah augmented their income by selling beer, presumably to the bargees on the canal (the premises later became the 'Bridge' public house). On the east side of the bridge lived Joseph Whitelegg, a coal dealer. He lived with his wife, Alice, their two teenage children and one servant. Near his house was the monument set up in 1790 by Dr. Charles White in memory of his father, after whom the bridge was named.

We shall consider the next section of Dane Road by looking first at the north side and then the south side. The first building on the north side of the road was 'Sale Priory', a large house built in 1711. It was set in its own grounds, surrounded by ornamental gardens and trees. Although Captain John White, the latest member of the White family, lived elsewhere in 1841, he still owned nearly 15% of the total area of Sale. This included the 'Priory', which was rented to John Frederick Foster, a Yorkshire-born barrister and magistrate with chambers in St. James's Square, Manchester. On the day of the census the Foster family were away from home, and only five servants appear on the list. The Foster family consisted of John (aged 46), his wife Caroline, and their three children. John Foster died in 1858. The 'Priory' was demolished in 1932 but the gardens remain as a public amenity.

The area near the junction of Dane Road and the modern Arnesby Avenue was called 'Pepper Hill'. Here were three houses, two of them being farms. The larger farm was rented by William Cookson from John Moore, who in turn leased it from Samuel Brooks. William was in his fifties and had a wife and eight children. His fields were scattered over an area which stretched from Broad Road to the River Mersey. The smaller farm was that of Martha Sutherland, a widow in her fifties. She rented two fields and an orchard next to the house. The other house was owned by John Carter. He was a cordwainer, and lived with his wife and three children. One of these was an apprentice cordwainer, and a second apprentice lived with the family.

The Pinfold was at the junction of Dane Road and Temple Road. This was where stray animals were kept until reclaimed by their owners and any damage done was paid for. The spot is still marked today by a triangle of grass at the junction. Opposite the Pinfold were two houses. The first house was the home of John Walkden, an agricultural labourer, who rented his house and garden from George C. Legh. John's wife and five children lived with him. Sarah Kelsall lived in the second house, which survives in an empty, dilapidated state. She was 68 years old and had three grown-up children and a servant living with her. She described herself as a 'farmer', but appears to have been a market gardener, as she did not have any land other than the garden next to her house. Dane Road Farm was the next building. This was run by John Singleton, who rented it from George C. Legh. John was around 60 years of age, and lived with his wife, one grown-up child and a labourer. The fourteen fields of the farm were scattered in an area from the east side of Old Hall Road to the Mersey. In addition John owned a house and large field near Baguley Road. The farmhouse in Dane Road is still lived in today. The last building on the north side of Dane Road was at the junction with Old Hall Road. In 1841 it was the shop of John Sheldon, a grocer. John was in his thirties; he and his wife, Martha, had four children and four servants.

We shall now look at the south side of Dane Road. The first building was 'Miry Gate House'. According to one directory this was built by Samuel Brooks, the Manchester banker. However, earlier maps, including the 1801 Legh Estate Map, show a house on the site, so it is possible that Brooks built a new house on the site for his friend, John Brogden, when the latter moved from Longsight to Sale in 1844. The occupier of the adjacent farm in 1841 was Joseph Cordingley. He was

38 years old and lived with his wife, two small children and two agricultural labourers. By the time of the Tithe Apportionment 'Miry Gate House' was occupied by Brogden, and Joseph Cordingley had moved to Temple Farm, at the end of Temple Road. John Brogden classed himself as a gentleman, and in the 1851 census we find that the name 'Miry Gate' had been changed to the more genteel-sounding 'Priory Gate'. The land rented by John Brogden included thirty fields leased from Samuel Brooks, two from John White and four from the rector of St. Martin's. Priory Road was known as 'Miry Gate Lane' and its name was changed soon after 'Miry Gate House' became 'Priory Gate House'. Along Priory Road we would see one farm, one house and a row of three cottages. Near Dane Road was the farm of Peter Brown. He lived with his wife, three children and four servants. The twenty-five fields of the farm reached from the south side of Northenden Road nearly to the Mersey. Next was a house approached by a short track near the modern Abbot's Close. With the two gardens adjoining, it was rented by John Hancock. He was in his fifties and his household consisted of his wife, Sarah, two relatives (?) and three servants. The three cottages on the other side of the road were known as 'Bancroft's Houses'. They housed three agricultural labourers and their families.

Clarendon Crescent, which was called 'Back Lane' in 1841, was not as straight as it is today. Along it there were two houses, the homes of three farm labourers with their families. One of the labourers, Peter Statham, unfortunately died four years later at the age of 35.

Opposite the house of John Walkden was the house of William Alderley, a wheelwright. He lived with his wife and a servant. It seems that a number of weavers and their families also lived in the house, making the total number of inhabitants 18. The house survives today. Near the Pinfold, in Finch Lane, was Temple Farm, which has also survived to the present day. At the time of the census, this was run by Thomas Barlow, who was 42 years of age. He lived with a housekeeper (and her three small children), three of his brothers (farm workers) and three other farm workers. He also had an elderly servant to help look after the household. Temple Farm consisted of thirteen fields, mostly in the neighbourhood of the farm buildings. In 1844 Thomas moved to Sale New Hall, and the Tithe Apportionment shows Temple Farm sub-let by Thomas to Joseph Cordingley. In addition to these rented properties, Thomas owned four houses and six fields in Sale, which he rented out to others. There were no buildings on the south side of Dane Road between Temple Road and Old Hall Road.

Appendix

Place names which were in use in 1841 and which have since changed or have disappeared

1841	1994
Back Lane (Ashton)	Glebelands Road
Back Lane (Sale)	Clarendon Crescent
Baguley Lane (Sale)	Baguley Lane & Road
Big Pit (Sale)	jcn. of Washway Road & Raglan Road
Boggart Lane (Sale)	Cromer Road, off Marsland Road
Broad Lane	Broad Road
Cabbage Row	row of houses in Chapel Road, near canal
Chapel Lane (Sale)	Chapel Road
Dane Lane	Dane Road
Davenport Lane	Rutland Lane
Dean Lane (Sale)	see 'Dane Lane'
Dean's Lane (Ashton)	Church Lane (west end)
Derbyshire Lane	Derbyshire Road
Finch Lane	Temple Road (north end)
Hart Lane	Northenden Road (Wythenshawe Road to boundary)
Hatters Lane	Harboro Road (south part)
Jacksmith Lane	Harboro Road (north part)
Macum Lane (Ashton)	Church Lane (middle part)
Marsh Lane (Ashton)	Carrington Lane
Marsland's Bridge	Brooklands Bridge
Massey Lane	part of Old Hall Road
Miry Gate Lane	Priory Road
Moor Lane	Northenden Road from Sale Bridge to Wythenshawe Road
Mosley's Lane	Derbyshire Road
Moss Lane (Ashton)	applied to both Moss Lane and Firs Road
Moss's Lane (Sale)	Wardle Road
New Lane	Marsland Road (between Derbyshire Road and Northenden Road)
Northen Road	Wythenshawe Road ('Northern Road' – with two rs – was used

	for parts of 'Moor Lane' in the 1860s)
Pepper Hill	area round junction of Dane Road and Arnesby Avenue
Sale Green	area round junctions of Dane Road, Old Hall Road and Broad Road
School Lane (Ashton)	Carrington Lane (between Ashton Lane and Firs Road)
School Lane (Sale)	School Road
Temple Lane	Temple Road
Wardle Lane	Wardle Road
White's Bridge	Dane Road Bridge

Bibliography

Primary Sources
Census returns, 1841, 1851, 1861, 1871
Tithe maps and apportionments for Sale, Ashton (St. Martin's), Ashton
(Bowdon), Baguley, Carrington, and Northenden.
Directories:
    Pigot, *Manchester, Salford and vicinities*, 1836, 1838, 1840;
    Pigot and Slater, *Manchester, Salford and vicinities*, 1841, 1843;
    Slater, *Manchester, Salford and vicinities*, 1845, 1848, 1851, 1852;
    Slater, *Directory of Cheshire*, 1844, 1850-1;
    Bagshaw, *Commercial Directory of Cheshire*, 1850, 1857;
    Slater, *Commercial Directory of Northern England*, 1848;
    White, *History and Gazetteer of Cheshire*, 1860;
    Morris, *Commercial Directory of Cheshire*, 1864, 1874;
    Kelly, *Post Office Directory of Cheshire*, 1857, 1864, 1906;
    Merrin, *Directory of Sale and Ashton*, 1910;
    Slater, *Manchester and suburbs*, 1888, 1891, 1893, 1894, 1896, 1897,
    1903, 1907, 1913, 1918, 1920, 1922, 1923, 1924, 1926
Parish registers for St. Martin's, Ashton-on-Mersey.
Sale Township Minutes, 1830-1848.
Sale General Rate Books, 1867-1880.
Burdett's map of Cheshire (1777).
Bryant's map of Cheshire (1831).
The G. Legh Estate map (1801), Trafford Local Studies Centre.
E. Mason's map of Sale (1806), Trafford Local Studies Centre.
Ordnance Survey maps, 1848, 1876, 1899, 1911.

Secondary Sources
Printed

A. Ingham	*Altrincham & Bowdon, with historical reminiscences of Ashton-on-Mersey, Sale and surrounding townships*, originally published 1879, second edition 1897, re-printed by Prism Books, Warrington, 1983.
J. Pipkin	*Cross Street Chapel, Cheshire*, H. Rawson & Co., Manchester, 1925.
H. Priestley	*The what it cost the day before yesterday book*, K. Mason, Havant, 1979.
C.J. Renshaw	*Some of the bye-paths in the history of the church of St. Martin's, Ashton-upon-Mersey, and of the Rectory,*

	1914, reprinted by Phoenix Press, Sale, 1950.
I.J.E. Renshaw	*Memorials of the ancient parish of Ashton-upon-Mersey*, W. Armstrong, Manchester, 1889.
	Memorials of nonconformity of Ashton-on-Mersey and neighbourhood, private publication, 1900. Copy in John Rylands Library, Manchester.
N.V. Swain	*A history of Sale – from the earliest times to the present day*, Sigma Press, Wilmslow, 1987, reprinted 1994.
M.D. Whitehorn	*The Story of Sale United Reformed Church 1805-1985*, Sale United Reformed Church, 1985. Copies in Trafford Local Studies Centre.

Unpublished

W.R. Burke	*Reminiscences of Sale*, unpublished manuscript, 1944. Bound copy of ms in Trafford Local Studies Centre.
H. Hulme	*Notes on the history of Sale*, unpublished manuscript, c.1950. MS 980 in John Rylands Library, Manchester.
E. Ogden	*Sale: one hundred years ago*, typescript, 1935. Trafford Local Studies Centre.
C.J. Renshaw	*Trees of interest in the old parish of Ashton-upon-Mersey and its neighbourhood* (n.d.), typescript, Trafford Local Studies Centre.

Newspapers

Sale and Stretford Guardian, 10 March 1950, 7 February 1958, 7 March 1958, 14 March 1958, 21 March 1958, 3 April 1958.

Manchester City News, 12 January 1895, 19 January 1895, 26 January 1895, 2 February 1895.

General Index
(please see separate name index for surnames)

Surname Name Index

Jerman 49
Johnson 53
Jones 35, 37, 38
Joynson 30
Just 23
Keighley 24
Kelsall ii, 34, 50, 51, 56, 58, 65, 70, 79
Leeds 60, 65
Legh 9, 50, 66, 70, 71, 79
Leigh 68
Lightfoot 59
Macome 45
Mainwaring 34
Malley 25
Marple 6, 68
Marsland 6, 15, 17, 33, 55, 56, 65, 66, 67, 68, 75
Massey 29, 61, 72, 76
Moore 5, 28, 30, 45, 71, 79
Moores 30
Morgan 76
Moxon 75, 76
Newport 43
Newton 8, 15, 40, 51
Nield 6, 31
Occleston 28
Ogden 54
Owen 21, 22, 46
Pattinson 34
Perrin 71
Renshaw 6, 23, 24, 34, 39, 47, 58, 67, 68, 72
Richardson 17, 25, 27, 30, 33
Roberts 28
Robinson 24, 39
Roebuck 25
Rowe 45
Royle 15, 24, 25, 42, 45, 46, 47, 59, 63
Shaw 59
Shawcross 8, 9, 50
Sheldon 79
Sherlock 51
Siddall 15, 20, 40
Simcoe 28
Singleton 39, 79
Skellan 65

Smith 8, 15, 33, 34, 70
Sowerby 46
Statham 80
Stamford and Warrington, Earl of 5, 8, 9, 20, 21, 22, 33, 50, 74
Stelfox 46
Stretell 76
Swain 2, 70
Sutherland 6, 68, 79
Taylor 9
Tonge 37
Topham 31
Trafford 71
Tyrer 6, 29, 66
Wainman 8, 9, 18, 20, 33, 34
Walkden 66, 79, 80
Wardle 63
Warren 17, 47, 59
Watson 43
White 8, 63, 72, 76, 78, 80
Whitehead 6, 67, 70
Whitelegg 8, 15, 39, 76, 78
Whittle 27
Williamson 27, 46
Winstanley 65
Wood 65
Woodall 39, 65, 67
Woodiwiss 9
Worthington 5, 72, 74
Wroe 45
Wright 9, 43, 45, 46, 56
Yates 23